Confectionery Design

by

L. J. Bradshaw

MEREHURST

LONDON

This edition published 1987 by Merehurst Limited,
Ferry House, 51–57 Lacy Road, Putney, London SW15 1PR
by arrangement with L.J. Bradshaw, 1 Thirlmere Avenue,
Orrell Post, Wigan, Lancashire WN5 8PT.

First edition published 1985
Reprinted 1988, 1989, 1990, 1992, 1993

© Copyright 1987 Merehurst Limited

ISBN 0 948075 76 7

Cover design by Clive Dorman

Typeset by Douglas Printers, Woodhouse Drive, Wigan, Lancashire

Printed and bound at The Bath Press, Avon

Contents

FOR MUM, RODNEY AND VALERIE.

Acknowledgements

I would like to thank Mr. R. O. Lace who initially provided me with the opportunity to enter the bakery and confectionery industry, thus allowing my fascination and eventually my creativity with edible materials to flourish.

My grateful thanks go to Reg. Oakes and Norman Hewitt for their expert tuition, guidance and continuous encouragement during my bakery studies at Bolton Technical College from 1971 to 1974

I would also like to convey special thanks to my Mother Reta Bradshaw for her constructive criticism and encouragement while writing the book, Miss Joan Russell ARCA one time Lecturer at the National Bakery School for her suggestions, Maureen Urquhart and Jean Melling for their speedy typing, and the Boots Company PLC, Nottingham and C & A for kindly giving me permission to use their logo designs.

Foreword

For many years excellent books have been published on the subject of cake decoration which have illustrated the practical aspect of this area of the confectioner's work. Such books have proved to be of great value to students and in particular to those who wish to specialise in wedding and celebration cake production.

While some authors have included chapters on the art of cake design none have approached this fascinating subject of depth, and now, at long last, a book has been published which provides a text with a practical approach to every aspect of the design of flour confectionery. The contents of the book also fulfil the requirements of the syllabus of the City and Guilds of London Institute 121 course which is offered in most Technical Colleges as a part-time course and also included on a full-time bakery course.

Mr. Lindsay John Bradshaw is well qualified to write such a book having taught this subject with considerable success to young and mature students in two major Colleges of Technology. His hobbies include painting, drawing and photography and he is keenly interested in competition work. He has won many awards at several national exhibitions and has also guided his students to notable success.

Since "Confectionery Design" was first published in January 1985, Mr. Bradshaw has continually endeavoured to improve and enhance its contents and substance. He has now been successful in producing this second edition with new additions, designs and photographs.

From my personal experience as a bakery teacher for over 30 years, it is my opinion that this book will prove to be invaluable to all who are interested in studying the art and design aspect of cake decoration and especially to students who wish to obtain a qualification in the subject.

J. G. FRANCIS
Former Head of Department
of Food & Home Economics
February 1987.   Salford College of Technology.

CHAPTER 1

Introduction to Cake Design

This book has resulted from my teaching experience, a most enjoyable interest, and an involvement over many years with the fascinating subject of confectionery design and decoration.

My initial aim is to provide a practical approach to the design of confectionery items, covering a wide range of techniques. I don't envisage that the book will make an artist out of you, however, it will demonstrate how to compile, execute and present a design specification for an article of edible confectionery. A definition of the word design for our purposes, could say that it is a compilation of artwork in the form of pencil line drawings, crayon or paint indicating a colour scheme mediums or raw materials to be used and in some cases reference to certain pieces of equipment such as piping tube numbers.

To have chosen to study this book as a relative newcomer, not so much to decoration but to design, the word design and more so the words painting and drawing can be a little daunting. So often I have discussed a cake decoration course to a prospective student and seen an obvious change in face when the design aspect is mentioned with a reply from the student such as "I can only trace, I can't draw" or "I could never paint at school". Don't let the word design deter your enthusiasm, you are not expected to be adept at fine art or graphics, (although a natural flair or even a serious interest in art will make things easier). However a knowledge of basic geometric principles and measurement are a distinct advantage. Geometric principles are dealt with in the book, so you can refresh your memory, or refer back when necessary. Even if you are familiar with these principles please read them.

Another requirement, the most important, is a sound knowledge and understanding of the edible materials available to you. With the exception of the occasional reference to certain decorative finishing materials I have not included any recipes or methods for the production of cake bases, creams or icing etc., as everyone usually has a favourite, or tried and tested recipe of their own.

In the case of the student new to cake design and decoration it is essential that one becomes fully aware of the possible uses, individual characteristics and limitations of each raw material, preferably before inclusion in a design specification or by using this book in synchronization with ones practical tuition or vice-versa. Flavours, textures, colour and consistency are just a few factors which have to be considered, for example it sometimes becomes difficult for students to decide whether a Royal icing inscription could successfully be directly piped onto a buttercream surface, when it would be better to first pipe the inscription on to a prepared sugarpaste plaque, which is then positioned onto the buttercream surface. Advantages using the latter method would include the fact that the sugarpaste would act as insulation between the "greasy" coating medium and the sugar piping medium, icing piped directly on to cream would eventually absorb, and be stained by the fat in the cream resulting in the original colour of the icing being affected. It can also prove to be difficult to pipe onto a soft cream surface.

Another example resulting from a lack of understanding of materials comes when deciding which side or base border to include on a fondant enrobed gateaux, once the fondant has crusted over it becomes a problem to try and mask a base edge of coconut or nib almond etc., therefore without a continuous production line employing sufficient operatives to carry out the process it could probably be more practical to edge the base with fondant piped bulbs, cut out marzipan pieces or piped or cut chocolate pieces which would be attached as a separate operation once the icing has set. So often I have seen students unaware of the qualities and limitations of fondant, design fondant gateaux with *fully* masked sides. This is in my opinion defeating the object of enrobing with such a superbly attractive coating medium and an unnecessary waste of skill (handling fondant) and a waste of material. Fully masked sides of nuts, vermicelli etc. are more usually associated with an initial mask or coating of adhesive material such as one of the many creams or preserves.

Basic elements of cake design always remain virtually the same, application, balance and layout etc., but with new trends, lifestyles and eating habits, development of new materials, and an increasing use of machinery, even in cake decoration, the confectioner needs to interpret design in a more modern form. Heavy and over elaborate design has now become a little outdated although it is often requested, usually by the more senior customer, mainly due to tradition and because the customer thinks they are receiving more for their money. The modern designer uses simple, clean, yet effective decoration, even so there will always be the customer who requires something a little more fancy than others.

Customers want variety when selecting a purchase of any kind, not only in the bakers shop but for instance when buying a new car, the model and often the colour takes priority. When choosing an item of clothing one needs variety to be able to select something which suits the occasion it is being worn for, whether it be plain or "dressy". Similarly cakes are chosen by the customer to suit an occasion or to incorporate within a meal or menu, the expected requirements or preferences of the palate. A plain oven finished type confection may be required to accompany one type of meal, whilst a very fancy elaborate cake would be necessary at a celebration, party or special presentation.

Texture and contrast also play an important part in satisfying a customers needs, for example choosing fabric, furniture and decor for interior design. To compliment or contrast in colour or texture also in the planning of a garden we also consider texture, colour and form to create a pleasing balanced effect. The designer confectioner uses crunchy, crispy, granular textures to compliment or contrast with smooth, stiff, creamy or jelly like consistencies.

Armed with this understanding of customer needs it is essential for the confectioner to display and offer for sale a varied selection of products from simple oven finished lines to the more highly decorated fancies and gateaux, adorned with icings, creams, fruits and nuts etc. This added finish we term decoration needs to be designed correctly to enhance the appearance of confectionery items, making them more appealing to the human eye.

Choice of materials used, (we established earlier) will obviously be governed by it's characteristics. Keeping and handling qualities being no exception this ultimately will determine the design possibilities. Chocolate, piping chocolate and fondant etc., need quick yet careful handling and are generally used for the quicker type finish or the more "everyday" type line. While Royal icing with it's longer drying time is used to produce fine delicate work whereas dairy cream has it's own special and indeed legal requirements which can somewhat affect and limit some potential design ideas.

Even so the majority of raw materials are incredibly versatile and open up to the confectioner a whole world of processing possibilitles, which include flavouring, colouring, moulding, cutting, rolling, texturing and piping to name but a few. Many materials will fall into two, three or maybe more of the afore mentioned categories, the possibilities are endless, and waiting for you to explore them.

When creating your designs always remember to DESIGN TO YOUR OWN PRACTICAL ABILITY, in other words don't choose to copy or create for instance a very intricatly piped design with a complicated colour scheme if your piping skills, or your ability to use colour correctly is insufficient to be able to reproduce and do justice to the design. Intricate, detailed designs requiring fine execution look very nice on paper, however you are the one that will have to manufacture that same specification in edible materials. It is far better then, at least until you become more proficient in practical skills to construct reasonably simple designs knowing that you will be able to easily execute them to an acceptable standard.

Enjoy your designing and have fun!

I have deliberately omitted from the introduction three terms referring to standards and styles of confectionery finishing, and which are frequently discussed and argued about by master bakers, lecturers and students alike, the terms being, COMMERCIAL, EXHIBITION AND COMPETITION. Everyone has their own views on which type or what standard of finish to confectionery should be termed commercial, and the dividing line or margin between commercial and what becomes exhibition style can be very wide. Needless to say I have not attempted to classify or categorise any of the designs in the book. I will say however, that the words STYLE AND STANDARD can confuse the issue even further in that one can try to emulate an *exhibition STYLE* slanted towards a commercially viable proposition, knowing full well that it is not of a sufficiently high quality of workmanship to be able to be classed as *competition STANDARD,* and unsuitable for entry in a competition.

Personally I feel that any item of confectionery produced that can be sold to make a profit is commercially viable. Several bakers do produce and sell with profit, highly labour intensive products such as very high class wedding cakes (often advertised as exhibition style), with run-out collars, handmade sugar flowers, even a build of linework using three or more lines. If a customer is

3

prepared to pay for that cake and the business person is making the required profit, then surely this and other examples must be considered commercially viable. The area location of a business expecting to sell this standard of work obviously plays an important part, the same exclusive, high class product, term it as you like, in some areas probably would not sell because of the high cost.

Items, designs and methods featured within the book will no doubt appear to some people as exhibition style finishes and one may feel they are too labour intensive to be produced within their own idea of commercial limitations, however, any design should be able to be adapted, simplified and made more cost effective without losing *all* it's appeal. Experiment a little, use your ingenuity. After all, that is what creative confectionery design is all about.

Wishing you every success!

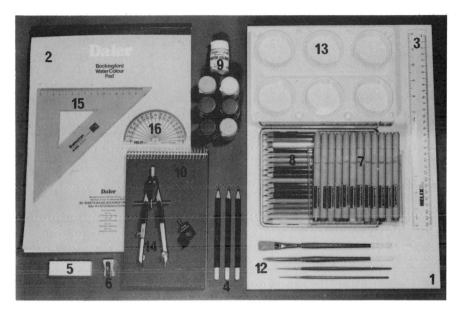

LIST OF DESIGN EQUIPMENT

1. ART PAD A3 SIZE (Cartridge Paper)
2. WATERCOLOUR PAPER PAD A3 SIZE.
3. RULER.
4. SELECTION OF PENCILS HB, 2H, 2B.
5. SOFT PENCIL RUBBER.
6. PENCIL SHARPENER.
7. FINE NIBBED FELT TIP PENS. Selection of colours.
8. COLOURING PENCILS.
9. POSTER OR GOUACHE PAINT: Spectrum Red, Spectrum Yellow, Ultramarine Blue, Burnt Umber, Burnt Sienna, Black, White - additional to these Flesh, Gold and Silver (available in poster only).
10. NOTE PAD.
11. GREASEPROOF OR TRACING PAPER.
12. SABLE BRUSHES No. 0, No. 1, HAIR No. 4, No. 8, $\frac{1}{2}''$ (13mm) CHISEL HEAD.
13. PAINT MIXING PALETTE See page 34.
14. COMPASS 14a Attachment to hold felt tip pen, useful for outlining.
15. SET SQUARE 45°.
16. PROTRACTOR.
17. OPTIONAL: DRAWING BOARD.
    RECOMMENDED: ART FOLDER See page 20.

CHAPTER 2

Geometric Drawing

It is useful for most aspects of cake design that the confectionery designer has a good, sound knowledge and understanding of geometric principles. Many cakes are based on a design using some form of geometry, whether they be round, square, octagonal, hexagonal, triangular, even down to the segments of a torte or large gateaux.

Instruments are necessary to execute the work accurately. The designer will require a supply of quality cartridge drawing paper along with a drawing board to work on (unless the art paper used is in pad form). Paper can be secured to the drawing board using drawing pins, masking tape or better still metal drawing board clips which will not deface finished artwork. Also required is a T square, set square, long ruler, a sharp medium hard pencil, pencil eraser, pencil sharpener and a compass.

THE CIRCLE Fig. 1

Names given to parts of the circle are as follows:

CIRCUMFERENCE   The outside line of a circle.

PERIMETER   Another term used to describe the outside line of a circle.

RADIUS   A straight line from the centre to the circumference of a circle.

DIAMETER   The line drawn across a circle passing through its centre

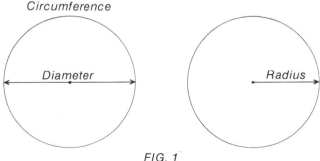

Circumference

Diameter

Radius

FIG. 1

The circle.

6

DIVISION OF A CIRCLE INTO 3/6 SECTIONS Fig. 2

The PERIMETER or CIRCUMFERENCE of a circle can be equally divided into six parts, by stepping out the radius of the circle around the perimeter it will divide into six times. By using the alternative divisions a circle divided into three sections will be obtained.

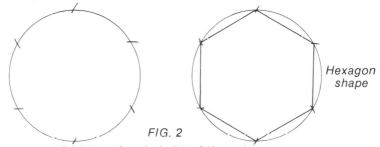

FIG. 2

Hexagon shape

Division of a circle into 3/6 sections.

DIVISION OF A CIRCLE INTO 2 AND 4 SECTIONS Fig. 3

To divide a circle into two equal sections, draw a line across the circle to cut through the centre point. To align the same centre line across the circle to be perfectly veritical or horizontal, and at a 90° angle to the paper edge, use the method described in Chapter 3, page 15.

The circle can now be further divided into 4 sections by using the distance A B as the radius on your compass, and with the compass point on A inscribe an arc above or below the circle, or both. Then with the same radius distance A B place the compass point on B and inscribe another arc or arcs to cut through the first ones made. Draw a line through the point of intersection and follow through the circle centre point, to form 4 equal sections each with 90° angles. If arcs are inscribed at the top and base of the circle simply draw a line through each point of intersection.

Fig. 3a illustrates an alternative method of obtaining 4 divisions within a circle, this time using a T square and a set square positioned on the centre line adjacent to the centre point.

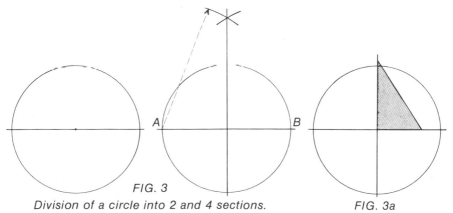

FIG. 3

Division of a circle into 2 and 4 sections.

FIG. 3a

BISECTION OF ANGLES Fig. 4

To further divide angles we use a technique referred to as BISECTION (to divide into two equal parts).

The angle we require to bisect as shown as VWX. The distance shown as Y is stepped out using a compass, this can be any distance just over approximately half the distance to be divided. The compass point is placed on W and an arc is marked, keeping the distance on the compass the same it is then placed on X and another arc marked. A line is then drawn from the point of intersection at Z to the centre point V thus dividing the angle into two equal parts.

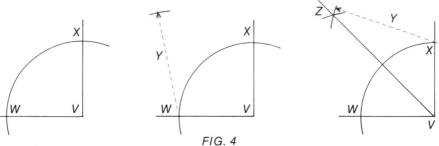

FIG. 4
Bisection of angles.

DIVISION OF A CIRCLE INTO MULTIPLES OF 3 AND 4

By using the principles described in figs. 2 and 3 which explain how to divide circles into 3, 6 and 4 divisions, we can now, with the aid of bisection techniques described in fig. 4 construct circles with multiples of 3 and 6 divisions as in fig. 5 and multiples of 4 divisions as in fig. 5a therefore enabling us to produce circles with 12, 24 and 8, 16 and 32 divisions respectively.

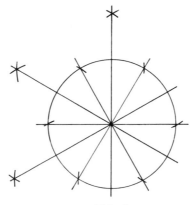

FIG. 5
Division of a circle into multiples of 3 and 6 using bisection.

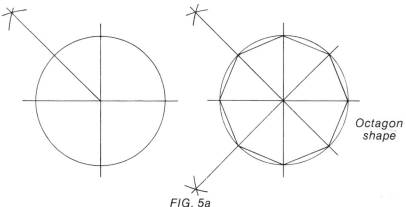

Octagon shape

FIG. 5a
*Division of a circle into multiples
2 and 4 using bisection.*

Bisection of circles is frequently used in cake design and in many instances when several divisions are made, a build-up of lines can occur close to the centrepoint as illustrated in the example fig. 5b. To avoid this, and eliminate eventual erasure of lines, only draw the bisecting lines into the centre of the circle as far as they are required fig. 5c, the length of the lines will depend on or be determined by the length of lines required to perform other constructional lines. Most of the circle area can be left reasonably clear for other details such as lettering or motifs etc., This method is particularly useful for anyone who should tend to 'press on' hard with a pencil when drawing, and of course find eventually that the same lines are difficult to erase cleanly without trace.

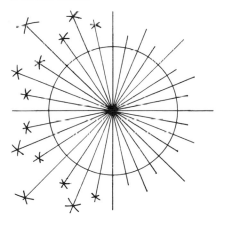

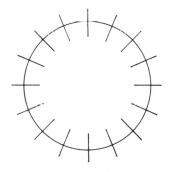

FIG. 5b

*Built-up of lines at circle
centre point.*

FIG. 5c

*Avoiding a possible
build-up of lines at
circle centre point.*

9

DIVISION OF A CIRCLE INTO
ODD NUMBERS OF SECTIONS Fig. 6

You may require to divide a circle into an odd number of sections, 5, 7, 9, 11 etc. We cannot use any of the previously mentioned angles because the numbers are divisable by two, therefore the following method should be used:-

The circle is divided in half with a line passing through the centre point, and cutting the circumference at V W. The line V W (DIAMETER) is then divided into the number of divisions required in the division of the circumference. The figure shows FIVE divisions.

The diameter of the circle V W is then stepped out from points V and W and two arcs are marked, where the arcs intersect at Y a line is drawn passing through the SECOND division on line V W cutting the circumference at X. The distance between V and X is then stepped out around the circumference using a compass. If the exercise has been carried out accurately, the circumference should divide into the exact number of sections marked on line V W.

Accuracy at all times and a sharp pencil are most important in this exercise.

Any number of division can be obtained using this method but the line Y X must always pass through the SECOND division on the diameter line V W.

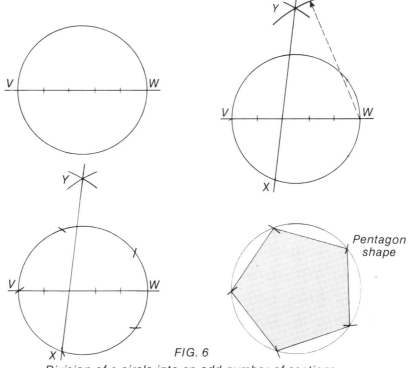

FIG. 6

Division of a circle into an odd number of sections.

DRAWING AN OVAL SHAPE Fig. 7

Draw the required width Z Y and depth X W of the oval intersecting the lines at O. With the centre point at O and the radius at O Z draw an arc to cut line W X at V. Next join Z and X together. Now using X as the centre and a radius of X V draw an arc to cut through line Z X, where the arc cuts at U bisect at U and Z. Draw a line through the bisection and cross at W. Where the bisection cuts line Z Y at point T and also at point W, use these points as centres for the arcs A and B. These arcs when joined will form an oval shape.

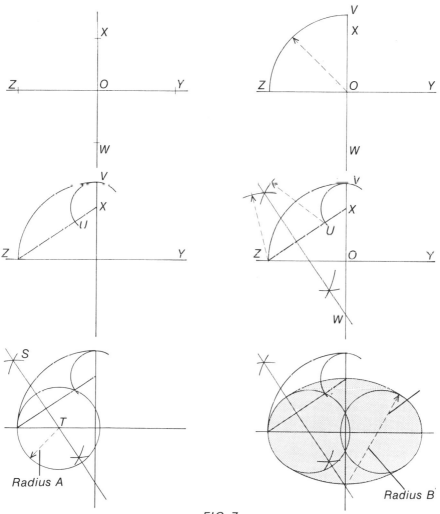

FIG. 7

Drawing an oval shape.

CHAPTER 3

Design Layout and Presentation

Before attempting to design any confectionery items let us first consider 'LAYOUT'. The designer should understand and realise the importance of layout in order that he can successfully present his finished work and hopefully project an image of being quite capable of creating and executing quality designs. Whether your designs are coursework as submission for a City and Guilds examination or whether you are involved in the development of new confectionery lines and the design ideas are to be considered by your employer for possible production, even if the work is for a visual lecture aid or simply to be used for display purposes, a balanced layout and clean, attractive presentation will carry several marks towards a higher grade in an examination and will most certainly hold your work in high esteem with your employer etc.

A pleasing layout will contribute towards improving a design that may not be totally balanced or coloured as attractively as you would have preferred. To achieve good layout, first consider how much information you intend to feature on your paper. In almost every design you will no doubt show a top view or as it is usually termed a 'PLAN' view, this is a view looking down onto the top surface of a cake, gateaux or fancy. You will appreciate it is inevitable that a plan view will always be necessary because of the fact that the main decoration of fancies, torte, gateaux and most celebration cakes usually focuses on the top surface of the item. A side view, or as it is usually referred to as 'SIDE ELEVATION' will be essential for most royal iced celebration cakes, which normally feature a large amount of side decoration and sometimes necessary to enable the indication on, for instance a gateaux, of a side masking of nuts, vermicelli, jap crumbs etc., or a side base edging of cut marzipan, cut or piped chocolate or any of the many piped borders. Constructional outlines for PLAN and SIDE ELEVATION are detailed later.

Besides the main plan and side elevation of a cake other information probably featured would be a title, the designers name and possibly a date, in the case of a student the class, group or section could be included. The other essential part to complete the project would be a write-up of product information, which usually incidentally could be kept very brief. We must therefore then arrange all the required aspects of a particular design to be centralized or appear to be evenly spaced on the paper with the relevant product information within easy access for reading with the design to create a pleasing appearance and convey a sense of continuity to anyone studying the finished work.

The "write-up", text, or product information, whatever you wish to title it as, should be brief yet giving sufficient data to enable anyone using the design to execute it in edible material or otherwise in practice with the correct materials, colours, sizes, shapes and piping tubes etc. Examples of these texts are given with each design from fig 38 to fig. 43. The text obviously acquires a more professional appearance if typed, however, neat, legible handwriting would suffice. The text should either be applied directly onto the art paper or by means of a separate sheet to be attached to the front or reverse of the design sheet.

Due to the enormous traditional popularity of round and square celebration cakes, plan views and side elevations for designs of such cakes will be the most frequently used. Fig. 8. For both round and square designs first draw a central line A B to equally divide the art paper in half and enable us to centralize the whole design. Next divide the width measurement of the cake size to be designed in half and use this same measurement one each side of line A B to draw two vertically parallel lines C D. Allow space along the top of the paper for the title of the assignment but more essentially to allow for the width of piped or run-out border to be included later, and then draw in a horizontal line E F with the aid of 'T' or set square to ensure accuracy. Measure down both C D lines the total width of the cake and draw in a second horizontal line G H this should then form a perfect square; the PLAN or top view of the cake.

A further horizontal line I J can be included here at the halfway width distance of the cake, to aid later design work especially necessary for corner run-out designing. Clear the bottom of the page and draw in two horizontal lines K L these should be spaced approximately $\frac{1}{2}$" apart to represent the depth of a conventional cake board. Measure up both lines D C from the top cake board line K L a distance equal to the depth of the cake, usually based on approximately 3", draw in the horizontal line M N to indicate the top edge or surface of the cake. The working drawing lines can then be erased if necessary or left until the design has been completed with borders, linework, lettering etc. Fig. 8d shows the PLAN and SIDE ELEVATION with working drawing lines erased.

Fig. 9 shows the construction of a plan and side elevation for a round cake. Start with a central line A B as for the square cake previously described, again allowing for the title and cake border, place a compass set at a radius equal to half the width of the cake to be designed and with the compass point on the centre line draw a circle. Place a set square on line A B with the right angled corner aligned to the circle centre point and draw in a horizontal line C D to pass through the centre point and cut the circumference in two opposite places as shown in fig. 9a. Where line C D cuts the circumference again align a set square as shown in fig. 9b and draw in a vertical line E F, repeat this on the opposite side, this will give us the width of the cake centrally positioned beneath the PLAN to enable us to construct the side elevation which is carried out using the same method as previously explained for the square cake. Fig. 9c shows the completed drawing with working drawing lines erased.

A similar basic layout to the two previous ones is shown in fig. 10a except for the size of the side elevation which has been reduced to represent the shallower sides of a torte or gateaux, note also the considerably reduced thickness of the cake board or in this case a cake card normally associated with torte and gateaux presentation. The centre circle is used to indicate the area usually allocated (approximately 3" diameter) to centre decoration of a torte see page 268 for examples. Using this basic outline, we can then divide the circle fig. 10c by means of bisection page 8 to indicate the segments of the torte in this case twelve. To vary or sometimes even improve and make your presentation more appealing figs. 10b and 10d show two alternative layouts for torten designs, both being particularly useful for separating individual torte segment designs. Also illustrated are examples of the positioning of product information. Fig. 11 shows construction of layouts for decorated swiss roll, battenburg, bar and layer cakes, note the differing dimensions for what are

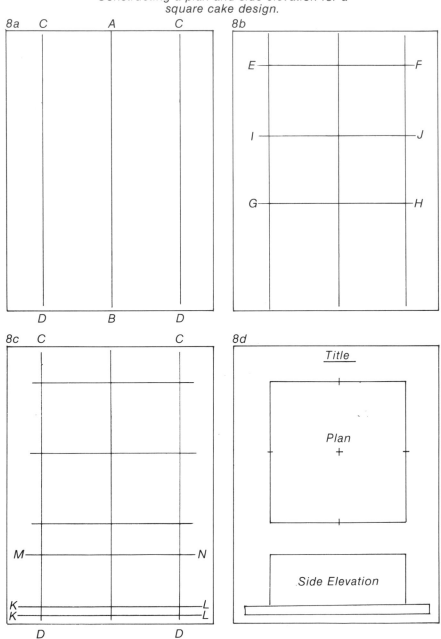

FIG. 8
Constructing a plan and side elevation for a
square cake design.

FIG. 9
Constructing a plan and side elevation for a
round cake design.

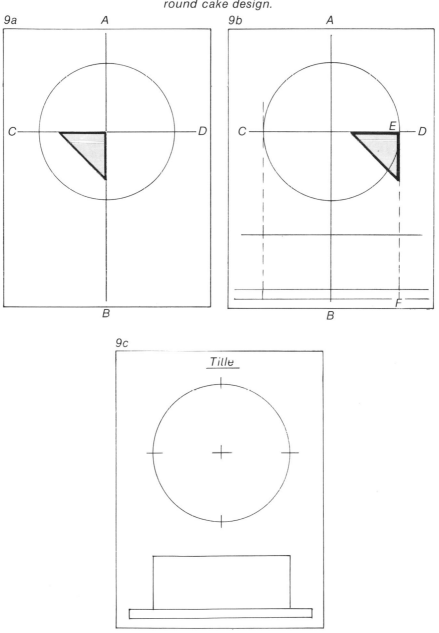

FIG. 10

10a, 10b, 10c constructing a plan and side elevation for a full torten design or torte segments.

10d constructing a plan and side elevation for torte segment designs.

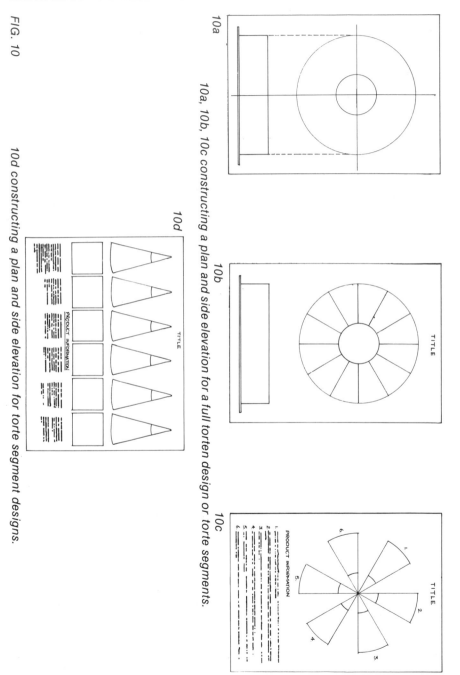

referred to as 'END ELEVATIONS' for the layer cake which are oblong shaped and the Battenburg based on multiples of squares. Torten and layer cakes are further dealt with in the design and motif section.

Fancies such as Jap, Fondant, Franzipan and Fresh Cream and any other of the smaller type confections you will agree always look far more attractive when arranged neatly and with a little thought given to the repetition or alternation of the design, colour or shape of the fancy displayed on a tray within a bakers shop window. If we were to 'mix up' a selection of colours, shapes and designs on the same tray, the effect would be 'bitty' and disjointed and therefore affect the visual appreciation and impact of each individual design. Repetition and alteration are frequently used methods of presentation by many of the higher class bakers and confectioners who have the initiative to extensively use window display to tempt the customer and hopefully sell more of his produce. Why not let effective window presentation influence and inspire your layouts for the designs of fancies. Fig. 12 shows alteration and repetition of shapes and designs, the same method can be used with the different colours of coating mediums determining the repetition or alteration - using these basics more permutations can be made to vary your layouts.

PRESENTATION

As mentioned earlier, good presentation contributes a lot to the sale of a product, the same applies to your finished artwork, not suggesting that you will initially be designing to sell for financial rewards but probably to gain marks in an examination and eventually develop designs for use in your own confectionery or celebration cake business or for your employers use. In all instances, it is essential to present your work as immaculately as you are capable of doing, in order to receive the anticipated results and respect for your work, so in effect you shall be using presentation to "sell" your designs.

A neat "uncluttered", clean and tidy approach is required throughout the entire design, from the unused sheet of art paper to the finished creation. Attempting to clean-up a soiled art paper can sometimes prove difficult in obtaining acceptable results and designs often have to be re-drawn because of unnecessary neglect.

Keep your hands and all drawing instruments clean, especially rules, set squares and protractors etc., which easily pick up pencil dust and smudge your paper, also keep food and drink away from your work to avoid splashes and greasy marks appearing. Other points such as tracing, erasing, use of correct pencils and titling etc., are dealt with in Chapter 5. Remember these hints and tips and you should produce what is normally required and accepted in the way of presentation.

Once you are satisfied that your design, layout and presentation is up to the standard you aimed for, then it is possible to still further improve the absolute final appearance, if cost allows that is, by covering your sheets of work with one of the widely available self-adhesive clear plastic covering films, the ones used for backing books and covering maps etc. If you haven't experienced applying the film to paper before be warned! your first encounter will very likely test your patience, it can have a habit of going it's own way and sticking where you may not want it to. I have heard of many instances when full sheets of artwork have been ruined by not applying the film correctly, so do read the

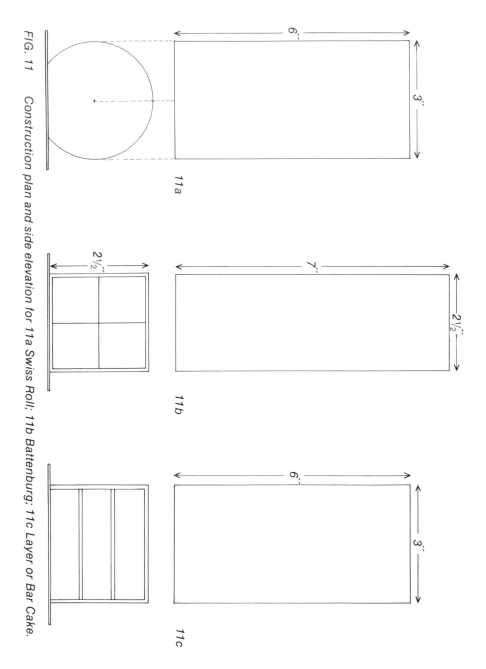

FIG. 11   Construction plan and side elevation for 11a Swiss Roll; 11b Battenburg; 11c Layer or Bar Cake.

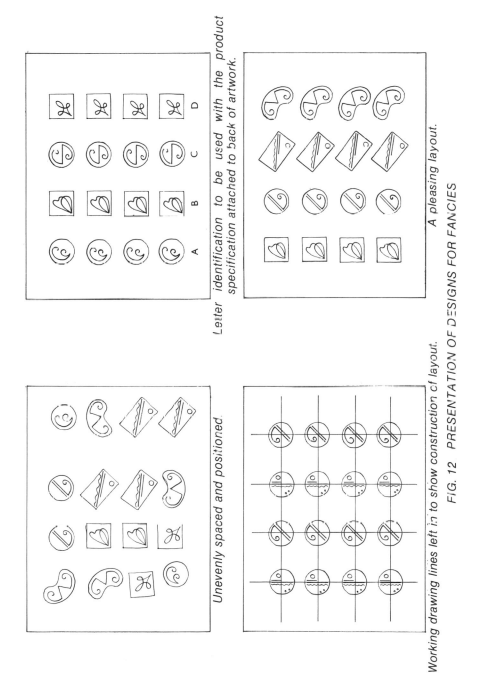

Letter identification to be used with the product specification attached to back of artwork.

A pleasing layout.

Unevenly spaced and positioned.

Working drawing lines left in to show construction of layout.

FIG. 12 PRESENTATION OF DESIGNS FOR FANCIES

instruction carefully before using. Successfully applied, the clear film certainly enhances designs and artwork, giving it a professional appearance with a slightly glossy surface (matt finish films are also available). The film also protects the paper against grease etc., which is especially helpful when using the design in the bakery, finishing or cake decoration room.

Designs, sketches, tracings which you intend to keep for further use and greeting cards, lettering examples and motifs can all be kept intact, and completely flat by storing them in an art folder. Art folders reduce the risk of creasing or tearing your artwork sheets, they are available in a wide range of qualities with prices to suit all pockets, from a basic stout board folder to one of the plastic types with zip fastener and carrying handle. Ensure when purchasing a folder that it will take A3 size paper, the size used for most of your larger designs. You can make your own inexpensive art folder, which would be quite adequate, by using the stiff card backs from two A3 sized art pads. Join the two cards together with strong tape or self-adhesive covering, the short used for shelves etc. Puncture two holes and thread some strong tape through to enable you to fasten the folder for carrying. Fig. 13. Three folded flaps made from thin card can also be glued inside as shown in fig. 13c to prevent papers sliding out whilst carrying the folder.

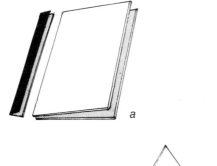

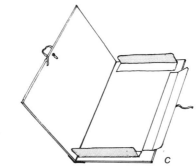

FIG. 13
Making an art folder.

CHAPTER 4

Colour Appreciation

The confectioner designer uses colour to make his products appeal to customers and therefore, hopefully sell them. A noticeable use of colour in the confectioners window is the association of various flavours with appropriate colours. The customer has become accustomed to, and takes for granted many colour associations and for instance would expect to find a pink coloured cake flavoured with raspberry, strawberry or perhaps cherry whether it be in the form of icing, cream, filling or even a liqueur soaked cake base.

Really the most important point for the confectioner to bear in mind is that all colour used should look edible. All colours of the spectrum except blue can be associated with natural food, the obvious association being that of fruit and vegetables, because nature uses them they are accepted as edible colours. However, colours which appeal to the human appetite in one food don't always appeal when used in other foods. We are tempted by the green of vegetables, orange carrots and red tomatoes but use these strong colours in any large amount for instance to coat a cake then they would look gaudy, laud and out of place. Tints of these colours are more successful for large areas. Blue is the only colour of the spectrum not used by nature in food meant for human consumption, even so used carefully for large areas in very pale tints will look quite acceptable. Full strength spectrum colours are used most successfully in small quantities; glace cherries, crystallized violets and angelica are all edible so their strong colours are accepted when used on a cake. Piping jellies and some jams have a transparent appearance and therefore can be used in greater amounts. Flowers, fresh and tinned fruit are all natural colours and become an easy way in which to introduce strong colour into your cake design.

So, the would be confectioner is faced with the questions what is colour? and how do we use colour?

Colour is reflected from light, the purest colour being from daylight. Light from the sun is composed of seven distinct colours in this order, known as the SPECTRUM:

VIOLET, INDIGO, BLUE, GREEN, YELLOW, ORANGE, and RED.

These true spectrum colours are known as HUES and can be observed by allowing a path of light to pass through a glass prism. the beam emerging from the other side will be the spectrum or band of colours. This band of colour can easily be seen in a rainbow.

Having said that the purest colour we see is by daylight from the sun, the confectioner must be conscious of the fact that he could be working under artificial light conditions, most electric light is deficient in blue light and therefore seems yellow tinged, some flourescent lights are deficient in orange/yellow and therefore give a blueish cold light. So colours will look different under these conditions opposed to daylight.

The colours used in confectionery are PIGMENTS as are gouache, poster, and watercolour paint etc., used by the artist. Pigments are materials used in the making of colours and paints, to explain; when we see something blue we see a colouring matter which reflects all the blue in the light falling on it, and absorbs all other colours. So yellow colouring matter throws back all yellow in the light and absorbs the rest. A black surface absorbs all the light and a white surface reflects back all the light.

Colour value should always be observed when cake designing. Colour value being the relationship with light to dark. Yellow, the lightest colour on the colour circle, has the highest value, and violet the darkest colour has the lowest value. Always try and use colours from light to dark otherwise the result will be a discordant effect. This will be dealt with later when discussing colour schemes.

PRIMARY COLOURS Fig. 14a See page 27.

These are three colours from which every other colour can be made. The three colours are: RED, YELLOW AND BLUE.

SECONDARY COLOURS Fig. 14b See page 27.

If equal quanities of any two PRIMARY colours are mixed together we get three other colours - ORANGE, GREEN and VIOLET. These are known as SECONDARY colours.

Primary		Secondary
Red and Yellow	=	Orange
Yellow and Blue	=	Green
Blue and Red	=	Violet

Arranged in the colour circle fig. 14 we can see the three PRIMARY and the three SECONDARY colours, also shown are intermediate colours between primary and secondary colours, these are known by the colours from which they are made.

TERTIARY COLOURS Fig. 14e See page 27.

By mixing two secondary colours together we obtain three other colours known as TERTIARY colours.

COMPLEMENTARY COLOURS Fig. 14b See page 27

Colours which appear opposite each other on the colour circle are said to be complementary to each other:

RED is complementary to GREEN
ORANGE is complementary to BLUE
YELLOW is complementary to VIOLET

TINTS Fig. 14d See page 27.

A TINT is a colour mixed with white. This can be seen in practical cake finishing when mixing colour into white icing.

SHADES Fig. 14d See page 27.

A SHADE is a colour mixed with black, not used excessively in cake decoration except in painting pictures and plaques etc.

USING COLOUR

A relatively easy way of using colour is a MONOCHROMATIC colour scheme, mono meaning one, chrome being colour. In this method only one colour is used therefore eliminating colour mixing and possible discordant effects. Provided the colour is added to one base material of the same degree of whiteness only. Normally one would start with a small amount of colour to white to produce a very pale tint using this to cover the main area followed by a deeper coloured tint for some of the decoration and finally a stronger coloured tint or even small amount of pure colour perhaps in the form of fine line piping or lettering/inscription. Remember, natural colour values light to dark, this has been executed in the monochromatic scheme.

Another popular form of colour application known as COMPLEMENTARY or CONTRASTING colour schemes uses colours opposite each other on the colour circle to produce some pleasing effects which are known to appeal to customers. Using the principle described previously one could start with tints of colour and then add a small amount of the colour complementary. Never use equal quantities of complementary colours, the result would be gaudy and "over-powering".

Usually the most difficult colour scheme to use successfully is colour HARMONY. Harmonious colour schemes are obtained when anything from three to six colours next to each other on the colour circle are used together. The colours however, must not be used at full strength otherwise the result again would be too gaudy. The colours must be mixed lighter but still following the natural colour value from light to dark to prevent obtaining a possible discordant effect. This is when two colours have been lightened and used next to each other but the light values have been reversed by the differing quantities of white. An example of discord would be an orange next to a lighter red-orange opposed to a lighter orange next to a darker red-orange which would create harmony.

COLOUR ASSOCIATION

When designing cakes and their possible colour schemes, always consider the association of colours with various themes, seasonal changes and occasions:

BLUE	We associate with coldness (blue with cold)
RED	Is warmth (Red Hot). Christmas.
PURPLE	Is associated with royalty.
YELLOW/ GREEN/ VIOLET	Together are thought of as Easter or spring colours.
RED/ORANGE/ BROWN	Together, make us think of autumn.

COLOUR APPRECIATION

In choosing a cake colour scheme, consider first a suitable base colour and then colours that you could successfully use with it to create a contrasting or complimentary colour scheme. As mentioned previously, monochromatic schemes are probably the easiest to use, however once we start using more than one colour, problems can occur. Also the use of some of the colours we use for decorative purposes on certain base colours can be very restrictive, therefore choose the base colour of your cake carefully when wanting to use multi-colours, motifs, cut-outs, painted plaques or other similar decoration.

White base colour and neutral colours such as coffee, biscuit and chocolate will accept all decorative colours, whilst mint green and pale blue base colours are more restricting in their acceptance of other colours. Pink, lemon and peach or apricot will accept most colours onto their surface.

The above paragraph is acting only as a very simple guide, and will be governed by such factors as:

      a.   Tint of base colour used.

      b.   Amount of each decorative colour used in comparison with each other.

      c.   Personal views and ideas.

CHAPTER 5

Drawing and Painting

A sound understanding of materials, ingredients and equipment is essential to be able to handle and utilize them in practice to their full potential. Similarly with the design aspect of cake decoration one must fully aquaint themselves with drawing and painting materials, their possible uses, characteristic effects and techniques. This chapter deals with pencils, poster and gouache paints, felt tip pens and pencil crayons thus enabling one to use them as effectively as possible to correctly draw, colourwash and add realistic detail to produce a complete design. Several useful hints and tips to make for easier drawing and painting are also included in the chapter.

PENCILS

All pencils are graded, grades being given to identify the degree of softness or hardness of each pencil. Hard pencils make thin light grey lines, whilst soft pencils make thicker dark grey or black lines.

Most good art shops offer a large range of grades, making it possible to obtain pencils from 6H extremely hard, to 6B extremely soft. The medium grade HB (Hard Black) or B is the most versatile for general use. The grade H and those beyond are the ones we require most, these being essential for the more precision work to execute accurate, crisp lines. Soft pencils are used more for sketching and tone drawings, they smudge easily and create a 'grubby' appearance to art paper if not used with care, likewise they erase easily, whilst the H range of pencils if applied with too much pressure being harder, become difficult to erase and can sometimes leave a slight indentation in the paper, so do ensure the line is definitely required before 'darkening' it. Grades 2H, H, HB and 2B are recommended for the book.

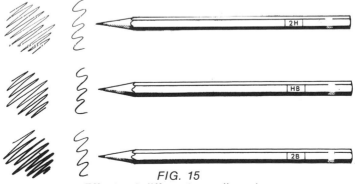

FIG. 15
Effects of different pencil grades.

ERASURES

When constructing designs and artwork it is advisable to use a soft 2B pencil, marking the paper very faintly, without undue pressure, thus enabling any eventual unwanted marks to be erased without difficulty. Once a satisfactory design is attained, the outline of the design, in other words all except the working drawing and construction lines can be outlined using a slightly harder pencil to produce a darker, fine line that will stand out from the rest. If the design is to be painted or crayoned then the constructional lines can be erased, leaving a faint outline to which one can work to when adding colour.

PENCIL CRAYONS

I personally do not advocate the use of pencil crayons for any large areas of colour, at least not for cake design purposes, although I do admire, favour and widely use them myself as an art medium generally. The book cover was coloured using this medium and as you can see produces an entirely different effect to paint.

If students sometimes wish to use them instead of paint, I usually recommend pencil crayons, only for relatively small areas of colour such as flowers, fruits, cherries and marzipan motifs etc. They are also ideal for anyone who finds difficulty in painting fine lines, being especially useful to indicate linework, ribbed rolling and to generally outline the edges of painted designs, provided of course that the pencils are used well sharpened.

The mention previously to pencil crayons not being used for large areas, refers to them being used to replace paint when colouring a large surface area to represent a gateaux or cake top, as it can sometimes be difficult to control an even amount of pressure being applied, resulting in 'patchy' uneven colours of light and dark tones. When using the pencils refrain from using undue pressure to avoid indenting the art paper surface.

PAPER

For rough sketches, outlines and layout ideas almost any drawing paper or sketch pad will suffice. When we come to actually preparing a line drawing or painted design for presentation then we should be a little more selective as to the quality and type of paper we employ.

For line drawing, a good quality cartridge paper should be used, it can be said the whiter and heavier the paper, the better the quality. Cartridge paper can also be used successfully for painting and colour washing, avoid however, using paper in block or pad form for this purpose as the paper may "buckle" due to the transfer of moisture applied when painting. To overcome the problem of buckling, cartridge paper can be used "STRETCHED", this is a process whereby the paper is first immersed in cold water for a few seconds (a clean sink is ideal), remove the paper from the water and allow most of the excess water to drip off. The wet paper is then laid completely flat on a wooden drawing board or other suitably sized piece of porous wood, not with a laminated surface. Gently sponge the paper from the centre outwards to the edges to remove all air pockets (visible as 'bubbles' or 'bulges' on the surface). Finally secure the paper onto the board with 2˝ (5cm.) wide gummed paper strip on all four sides, with approximately ½˝ (13mm.) of the strip

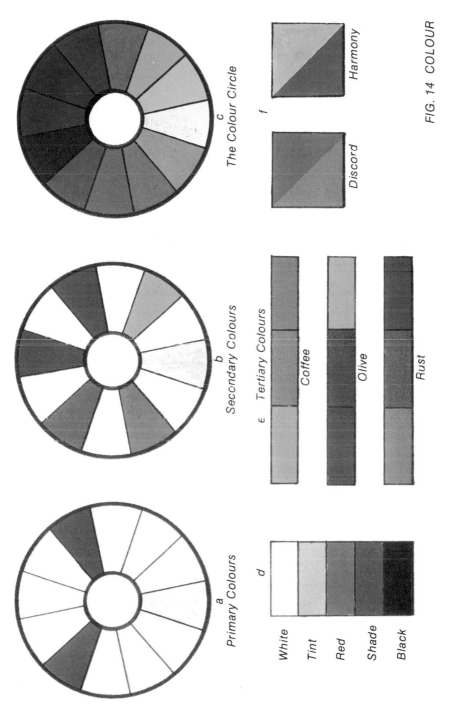

a
Primary Colours

b
Secondary Colours

c
The Colour Circle

d
White
Tint
Red
Shade
Black

e Tertiary Colours
Coffee
Olive
Rust

f
Discord
Harmony

FIG. 14 COLOUR

27

*Painted edible fruits, flowers,
nuts and decorations.*

28

attached to the actual paper, allow the paper to dry naturally. Do not try to accelerate the drying process by using artificial heat, this usually results in uneven drying.

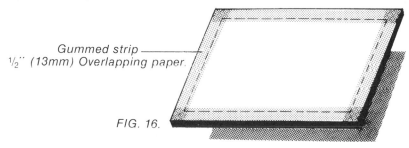

Gummed strip
$\frac{1}{2}''$ *(13mm) Overlapping paper.*

FIG. 16.

Once the paper is thoroughly dried it is ready for use, and should not "buckle" when moisture is re-applied during painting.

The equipment and materials list on page 5 gives watercolour paper as optional, it is considerably more expensive than cartridge paper, however, for painting, watercolour paper provides for a superior alternative to cartridge paper both in practical use and presentation qualities.

Ideally all watercolour papers should be stretched before use, unless the process has been carried out by the manufacturer. Use the same method described previously. I use DALER BOCKINGFORD paper, this is in pad form which I separate for use. Individual sheets can be purchased at most good art shops.

At this stage I hasten to add a little reminder, to avoid wasting valuable materials, only use watercolour paper for painted designs of which you know are correctly and accurately drawn and balanced, and that are to be coloured with a scheme known by yourself to work reasonably well.

I should imagine you will remember this reminder after purchasing your first stock of watercolour paper.

The most useful sizes of paper for confectionery designs are the following:-

A3 -
$11\frac{3}{4}''$ x $16\frac{1}{2}''$ (297mm x 420mm)

Essential for plan and side elevations of torte gateaux and wedding cake and celebration cakes.

A 3

A4 -

$8\frac{1}{4}''$ x $11\frac{3}{4}''$ (210mm x 297mm)

Convenient size for sheets of motif illustrations, cake tops, lettering, and small fancies, etc.

A5 -

$5\frac{7}{8}''$ x $8\frac{1}{4}''$ (148mm x 210mm)

Handy for small sketches, quick drawings and notes from demonstrations, window displays and blackboards, etc.

A2 -

(double A3 size), or larger may be required for full base tier drawings and large presentation cakes.

COLOUR APPLICATION

Throughout your application of colour onto drawn designs always use the colours of the paints and felt tip pens as if they are the edible materials being employed in the practical manufacture of that particular design. Imagine the colours as creams, icings and jellies etc., this will help considerably when preparing and mixing colours to paint with, being especially useful when colour washing (described later) a design to represent a coating of royal icing, buttercream or fondant etc. The white base paint with which you start, as being the white royal icing, cream or fondant. To this you would be adding paint to obtain the required tint, in this case the coloured paints would represent food colourings or colour-flavour compounds. Using this method you will obtain edible looking colours of the correct tint, rather than gaudy pinks or yellows etc. Once you have prepared, what you consider to be an acceptable colour, apply some of the paint over a small area on a spare piece of paper or better still if economics allow, paint an area of similar shape and if possible size to that of the design to be painted, this can then be used later to experiment on with other prospective colours for lettering, motifs, flowers and linework etc. The object of painting the colour and allowing it to dry previous to using it on the actual design is to enable you to examine the paint colour in the dry state, which could vary lighter or darker, depending upon such factors as the amount of water used to dilute the paint, different types of paper and thickness of application etc. Going back to the idea of using colouring materials as if they are colours of edible materials, the same would apply to the use of felt tip pens, these could first be tested on your already 'test painted' area and applied in various thicknesses and with varying amounts of pressure and overlapping until the desired effect is obtained before being transferred onto the main design.

COLOUR WASHING

The term 'COLOUR WASHING' used in confectionery design refers to the process of applying paint to a given shape to create a background for further design, the background in effect representing the recommended coating medium and colour for the particular cake being designed, usually royal or water icing, fondant, buttercream or dairy cream etc. The paint is usually based on white with a colour tint added, except for colours used to represent chocolate coatings or enrobing. Two popular methods of applying colour washes with poster or gouache paint are described below:-

STENCIL OR BRUSH APPLICATION

For both methods mix an amount of white paint sufficient for the area to be painted, allowing for a test paint, gauging quantities of paint required will become more accurate with experience. The white paint is mixed with water, adding a little at a time with a paint brush until a consistency similar to that of unwhipped whipping cream is obtained. Too much water would thin the paint excessively and produce a transparent finish, similar to a watercolour painting, while insufficient water would render the paint thick and difficult to apply successfully without probably leaving brush marks and possibly drying before the washing process is completed, resulting in a 'patchy' finish.

STENCIL APPLICATION

This form of application is probably the quickest to complete, that is once the stencil or template has been produced. Using mostly standard sizes of torte, gateaux and fancies etc., one stencil cut-out for each could be used

FIG. 17
Card templates for stencil type application of a colourwash.

repeatedly, providing it is cleaned, dried and stored flat after use. The stencils or templates are used to create a background as mentioned earlier, so simple square, round and oblong shapes are all that is required. Draw the required shape onto the chosen stencil material and then cut out the shape using a sharp knife to ensure a clean cut edge. The best material to use is oiled parchment which is moisture proof, and available from most good art and craft shops. In the case of a 'one-off' design shape, thin card or even cake box card can be used successfully, but would be unsuitable for any excessive use. Further information on stencil work is given in chapter 12.

Place the stencil completely flat on the art paper. holding it firmly with all fingers and the thumb and then with the other hand apply the prepared paint with the aid of a small piece of foam sponge swiftly and evenly in broad strokes across or down and over all the template edges therefore completely

filling in the shape, fig. 18. Carefully remove the template and allow the painting to dry before further work is carried out. On removing the template, if found that an uneven edge has been formed this can be thinly outlined with a fine nibbed felt tip pen of the same colour to neaten the edge, otherwise if being used, a masking or border design would eventually cover it.

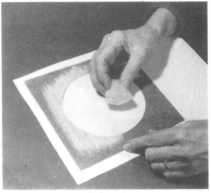

FIG. 18
Stencil template in position, a small piece of foam sponge is used to apply a colourwash.

BRUSH APPLICATION

Having prepared the design outline, one of two methods can be used. The choice of method will depend upon the intricacy of the outline. If a simple round, square or oblong shape is to be painted then one brush can be used, to both outline and fill in the area with paint.

For gateaux designs from around 5" upwards, torten and layer cake designs, I find a $\frac{1}{2}$" (13mm) chisel head brush ideal for this purpose. A number 8 brush could also be used. For smaller areas such as designs for fancies, a number 4 brush or even smaller number 2 would offer greatly improved brush control.

Follow the outline carefully using the prepared paint and then with a swift action brush evenly from side to side of the outline to completely fill the shape.

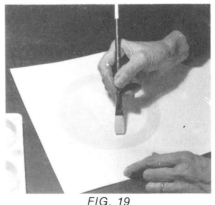

FIG. 19
A colourwash applied using an $\frac{1}{2}$" (13mm) chisel head brush.

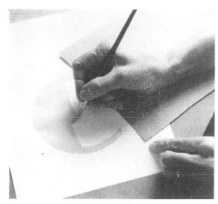

FIG. 20
A colourwash can also be applied using a number 8 brush.

FIG. 21
To facilitate easier outlining of designs after painting, make a card template incorporating the required shapes.

The second method employs two brushes. This method is used when the design background is a little more intricate or involved than just a plain square or circle, for instance if an area of white is to be featured on the design to indicate say, a sugar paste plaque, this white would be difficult to paint over a coloured background, so one would normally outline around that particular area with the painted colour wash and leave the white art paper exposed. To use large brushes as previously described could prove difficult around these small areas so for this type of colour wash, outline first using a small brush number 4 or smaller number 2 around the shape and the intricate areas and then have at hand a number 8 or number 4 brush to continue the filling in operation as before. Some people find it easier to slightly tilt the drawing board which is holding the art paper by raising it upon a suitable object in order to help and allow the paint to flow down the paper and make for easier washing. It is up to the individual to experiment with all methods of colour washing until one achieves the best results.

FIG. 22
To indicate white areas on a design, paint around them and colourwash with small brushes, then finish with larger brushes.

33

Always ensure and double check that all dimensions, spacing, and positioning of motifs etc., are absolutely correct before commencing to colourwash, or add colour in any other way as it is difficult to alter any drawing errors once the colour has been applied.

When colour washing large areas, ensure that sufficient paint has been mixed for the design and a test paint before starting the process. It is far better to have a little mixed paint left over than having to mix more paint and try matching it to the original colour used, during which time the initial application would have dried therefore probably resulting in a joining line being noticeable when finished.

One final point to note when colour washing, avoid over loading the brush with paint, as this may accidently be released when not required and result in flooding the painting.

Once the background colour has dried, the next large area of colour can be painted on. This can be seen in fig. 23, where an area of green is being added to indicate a rib-rolled marzipan easter-egg shape, the rib-rolling would then be shown on the design by drawing in parallel lines with a felt pen of a slightly darker colour than that of the marzipan background to emphasise the texture and shadow that would be created in practice.

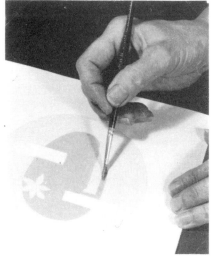

The painting is further finished by the painting or drawing in of lettering, flowers, leaves and linework etc., to complete the design which can be seen on page 44a.

To facilitate easier mixing of paint colour and help to keep paint pots clean, with no foreign colour present, use a wooden cocktail stick to remove a small dab of colour from the paint pot or tub onto your paint palette.

FIG. 23

Once the base colourwash has dried, other colour and detail can be applied. Note the areas left white to represent sugarpaste.

Colour that you use frequently, or colours which are time consuming and difficult to mix to the correct tone can be prepared by mixing a large amount and storing in clean redundant paint pot containers. Don't forget to label them. Some useful colours to prepare in advance are flesh colour, leaf green, lilac, and 'biscuit' colour for colour washing.

Paint palettes can be purchased from all good art shops, and will serve you well providing you clean them thoroughly after each use. Don't allow the paint to dry or harden as it becomes more difficult to remove.

Home-made palettes are easily provided by using empty polystyrene egg boxes, which are waterproof. Use both halves, the 'egg shaped' half is readily sectioned for small colour mixings, whilst the plain oblong half is ideal for a water holder or as a palette for mixing large amounts of colour for colourwashes. Plastic margarine and yoghurt containers also make excellent palettes (remove all traces of grease with hot soapy water). Save the plastic tops from aerosol cans, as these make good water containers. The advantage of all the afore mentioned palettes and pots is the fact that they cost nothing, and when they get past their best, there's no need to wash them, simply dispose of them!.

Adding the smallest amount possible (tip of the paintbrush) of dishwashing liquid to your prepared colourwashing mixture will help considerably the flow, smoothness and application of the paint.

COLOUR MIXING HINTS

Chocolate Colour

When mixing paint to represent chocolate on a design, use a base of burnt umber or burnt sienna with a little spectrum red added, this will reproduce a rich, more edible looking brown colour. This is a similar practice to the one used in the bakery, that of adding pink food colour or red compound to chocolate cake mixes to improve their appearance.

The choice of burnt umber or burnt sienna will depend on whether a milk or plain chocolate colour is being depicted.

Very little IF ANY white paint should be used when making chocolate colour

Green Colour

Green colour will also be enhanced and made to appear more of an edible type colour by the addition of extra yellow, to give a nice pistachio type of green colour.

Flesh Colour

Flesh colour for painting designs of marzipan motifs, plaque paintings etc., can be obtained by starting with a base of white paint, then adding a combination of orange or red and yellow and a little brown, the combination will depend upon whether a natural or cartoon like flesh colour is required, experiment yourself, note the combinations used alongside a sample of each colour and keep for future reference.

Coffee Colour

Here a little experimenting will be required to produce a coffee colour acceptable to yourself. Try a combination of white, brown and a little orange, or for a different tone mix quantities of orange and green together as used to obtain a tertiary colour on the colour mixing chart, fig. 14e, page 27.

Peach Colour

Based on orange (red and yellow) with a little extra pink (red and white) then add white to give the required tint.

Apricot Colour

Again based on orange (red and yellow) with a little extra yellow, then add white to obtain the tint you require.

HINTS AND TIPS

SYMMETRICAL MOTIFS

Symmetrical motifs can be made easier to execute more accurately by first drawing the shape of one side of the image, this can be any side of a vertical or horizontal line (depending on the drawing). Having perfected the shape to your liking it can then be outlined on to tracing paper, reversed, and then aligned exactly opposite the first half of the image to be carefully copied, completing the full image. Page 261 shows an example of this technique in use.

UNIFORMITY

To ensure uniformity, any part of a design which needs to be repeated elsewhere on the same plan, such as rosettes of cream on torte segments, fruits, marzipan motifs or repeated inscriptions, these should be accurately reproduced, this can be done by first preparing the drawing to be repeated on a piece of scrap paper, in this way one can perfect the work before including it on the final artwork. Outline this drawing on to tracing paper, position in the correct place and copy the drawing as many times as necessary. Even though for instance fruit and rosettes of cream would naturally vary slightly, this exercise is particularly important in creating a well proportioned and executed piece of artwork.

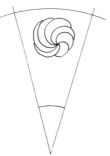

Make a tracing of the motif shape with some form of re-positioning markers, shown here as dots.

Draw the required motif shape in the correct position, in this case a cream rosette on torte segment.

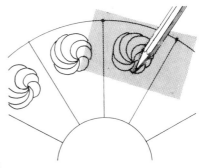

Re-trace as and where required, by aligning the dots on the tracing in the correct position on the design, shown here as the corner of each segment.

FIG. 24

SHADOWS AND HIGHLIGHTS (See page 38)

To enable easier and more accurate positioning of shading and highlights on painted designs and motifs, draw a small arrow in pencil in a corner of the art paper, this will continually serve to remind you when painting, from which direction the light is appearing. The shadows can then be painted on the opposite side of the image to the one that the arrow is pointing at. Highlights of reflected light would be painted on the side of the unit or surface opposite the shadow and nearest the arrow point.

Application of Shadows and Highlights

A.   Draw the motif to be shaded and highlighted, also include an arrow in a corner of the art paper to indicate the direction of light.

B.   Make a tracing of the motif and move it across the drawing at the same angle, and in the same direction of the arrow, the distance moved will be determined by the amount of shading required. Now draw over the tracing of the motif in the second position.

C.   Leave all the pencil lines in that are required to paint the shading, use imaginary lines (shown dotted) to determine which shading outlines are required.

D.   Erase all unwanted lines.

E.   Paint in the shading, in this case around one side of the marzipan flower.

F.   Paint in the shading around the flower centre. Note how a light and a darker shade have been used to emphasize the roundness of the royal icing centre bulb.

G.   Now paint in the highlight or light reflection, nearest to the arrow point.

H.   Using the same areas as the initial shading, the thickness of the marzipan is indicated by using a darker shade around one side of the flower edge.

Finally erase the pencil arrow.

To paint shadows on cake surfaces, or indicate the thickness of sugarpaste and marzipan by the use of shading use the same colour as the surface, motif or material and add a small amount of brown or brown and blue mixed together to form a dark grey, the amount of brown or grey added will depend on the degree of shadow cast required.

Highlights or light reflections are painted with pure white, or a combination of white with a little of the unit base colour depending on the type of surface being indicated. Use highlights on cherries, piping jelly, fondant and chocolate etc., to emphasize their shiny, reflective surfaces.

A.

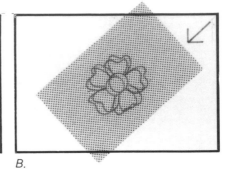

B.

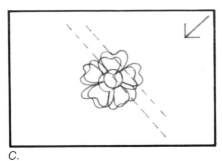

C.

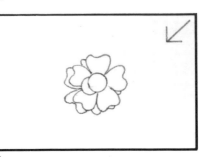

D.

E.

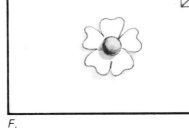

F.

G.

H.

CLEAN APPROACH Fig. 25

When drawing and especially when painting it is advisable to use a piece of clean paper between your artwork and your hand that is resting on the paper, this will assist in keeping a clean appearance to your work, helping also to prevent soft pencil and paint smudges also moisture or grease smears from your hands transferring on to the art paper.

TRACING Fig. 26

Tracing can become very tedious, especially if the drawing being traced is of an intricate nature. Keeping the tracing paper correctly in position, holding the paper and using a pencil is easier if the tracing paper is held in position with small pieces of masking tape applied with the minimum of pressure so as not to deface the art paper on removal, this leaves you free to trace more accurately, also the work can be left and finished off at a later date without fear of the tracing being moved.

FIG. 25

Work cleanly, avoiding soiling your art paper by using a piece of paper between the art paper and your hand.

FIG. 26

To facilitate easier tracing, use a small piece of masking tape applied with light pressure.

FIG. 27.

Linework is easily indicated on a design by using a fine tipped felt pen. Should pen colours react with paint to produce unsatisfactory colours, use a number 1 or number 0 brush with poster or gouache paint.

FIG. 28
*Small decoration and detail can then
be painted on.*

RIBBED ROLLING

To indicate ribbed rolling of marzipan or sugarpaste on a design simply draw in horizontal, vertical, diagonal or criss-cross (boxwood roller) lines using a fine felt tip pen of a darker colour than that of the base colour used to indicate the marzipan.

Diagonal   *Vertical*   *Boxwood*   *Basketweave*
              (or Horizontal)

FIG. 29. *Indicating marzipan and sugarpaste textures.*

DRAWING CURVES

To aid the drawing of curves, especially on painted designs where a mistake could be disastrous. Try using a template fig. 30. The curve is first drawn on to a spare piece of paper until the desired shape is obtained, then a card template of the curve is cut-out, (use "cake box" card), align the template in the correct place on the design and outline the shape with a pencil or felt pen of the required colour. This technique should be repeated or reversed, even for a single curve, it reduces the risk of drawing a 'wobbly' line so often seen with free hand drawing.

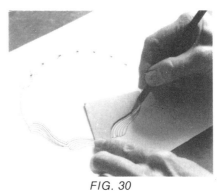

FIG. 30
*Repeating a curved shape is made
easier with the aid of a card template.*

SILVER AND GOLD CAKE BOARDS

To enable a realistic effect to be obtained when painting in a cake board edge, cake band, and plastic cake decorations such as horseshoes, a silver or gold coloured poster paint is available, thinned with water as for other poster paints and easily applied. After use brushes are cleaned using water, unlike other metallic paints which require turpentine for cleaning brushes.

Silver and gold bands can also be indicated on a design by gluing a piece of the actual cake band on to the art paper. I would not however recommend using velvet ribbon in this way as the finished effect takes on a "collage" type appearance and would be unsuitable for covering with clear plastic film (described on page 17).

USING TEMPLATES FOR OUTLINING

Irregular shaped or intricate design outlines, other than basic geometric shapes that are to be repeated, can be drawn quicker and more accurately by the use of card templates. These templates are very useful when compiling a sheet of for example fresh cream or frangipan fancies. Simply draw the required shape outline onto thin card, cut-out with a sharp craft knife, position onto your art paper and draw round the inside edge of the template with a pencil. Markers could be included on the template to assist correct alignment of the shape within a layout. If the design is to be painted the template can be further utilised to outline the painted design with a fine tipped felt pen

FIG. 31
Using a card template to accurately repeat irregular shapes, shown here being used to prepare a sheet of sponge finger based fancies.

FIG. 32
A sheet of frangipan fancy pastry outers, repeated with the aid of a template and then painted.

FIG. 33. USING CARD TEMPLATES

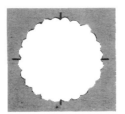

Frangipan fancy template with markers.

Sponge finger or eclair template with markers

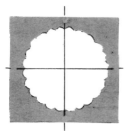

Template markers aligned with layout lines on art paper.

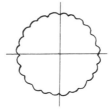

Outline drawn, and template removed.

Inside edge of pastry case indicated with a circle.

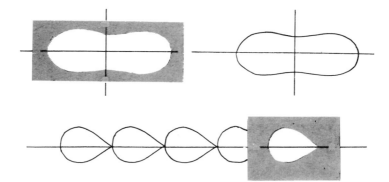

Using a card template to draw a piped shell border outline.
Similar techinque could be used to draw a border on a curved line.

Working drawing line erased.

 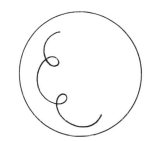

FIG. 34

Using a card template to draw curved   Line drawn onto the design. The
linework on a design, use with pencil,   same card template could be used as
   felt tip pen or pencil then paint.   a guide to pipe linework onto actual
                                              cake top.

TITLES

Finished cake designs will be easier to **refer** to and select if titles are added. Keep the lettering used for the titles and your name neatly positioned at the top or bottom of the art paper. Use two straight guidelines to print the necessary information, or for a more professional appearance use a plastic lettering stencil with a fine felt tipped pen, or dry transfer lettering such as LETRASET which is available in many styles and sizes.

Title using a
Stencil set

Title
using
LETRASET

43

CHAPTER 6

Design Techniques

The word design refers to a drawing or plan that shows how something, in this case an item of confectionery, is to be made, a general form or arrangement of lines, shapes and lettering to create a complete decoration. To be successful a design should convey an appearance of overall balance and completeness. The two types of balance we can employ are termed as SYMMETRICAL and ASYMMETRICAL.

Symmetrical fig. 35 means that all parts should correspond in size, shape and position on either size of a dividing line or round a centre, this type of design is more suited to items of confectionery which can be sold both as a whole unit or segmented such as a torten or layer cake which can be sliced to allow an individual section of a complete design to be removed without fully losing the theme of the whole design. Symmetrical designs are normally easier to design and to achieve overall balance with. However, they can be more time consuming and labour intensive to reproduce in practice, because of the necessary degree of accuracy required to execute the design on each segment or slice as near exact as is practically and if applicable, commercially possible. A design intended to be symmetrical that has not been executed correctly can look very untidy.

Asymmetrical design, fig. 36 is usually considered the more difficult type to design but in practice will tolerate less accuracy to a certain extent, especially on mass production, this does not mean that the usual necessary care in practical execution need not apply, but that we can allow slight variations without them being too conspicuous. Asymmetrical designs are more suited to confectionery items which are offered for sale only as a whole unit, otherwise when sliced or segmented and sold separately the design would be meaningless.

FIG. 35. Symmetrical design.

FIG. 36. Asymmetrical design.

EASTER GATEAUX

Orange genoese base layered with buttercream and orange curd or apricot jam. Coated with pale orange coloured fondant. Base border of rib-rolled green marzipan semi-circles. Top decoration, rib-rolled green marzipan egg shape, edged with chocolate coloured scratched line. Directly piped chocolate stems with white royal icing 'pussy willow' and moulded or piped daffodils, violets and leaves. Sugarpaste plaque with directly piped lettering.

44a

ALMOND

COFFEE

44b   *Layer cake tops*

As mentioned earlier, symmetrical designs are usually in favour as being the easier type to design and balance, due to the fact that the arrangement of decoration is repeated at least once as a direct opposite, or several times as part of a segmented design. It can therefore be difficult when one reverts to designing asymmetrical layouts to achieve any form of balance whatsoever.

A balanced asymmetrical design.

Asymmetrical design with incorrect layout resulting in an unbalanced effect.

To help avoid unbalanced designs one can base the form of decoration around a number of different layout determining lines, these lines in practice would obviously be reproduced in some form of edible material for example, piped buttercream, or royal icing lines, fondant, chocolate or a strip of marzipan, even rib rolled for extra dimension. The lines would then form a basis for you to build upon, using other edible materials such as jelly slices, nuts, cherries and other glace fruits, chocolate pieces, marzipan figures and lettering etc. The time and labour involved in producing these types of confectionery designs is normally associated with "keeping" lines and weekend specials, they are not normally found on for instance dairy cream coated gateaux with fresh fruit decoration, the bases therefore would be high ratio, butter sponge or good quality genoese coated with buttercreams, fondant, chocolate and decorated with items such as those mentioned above. Examples of layouts are shown in fig. 37. It can be seen that the lines are used singly or two, three or four together, both straight and curved and in combinations of straight and curved. The most useful I find, is the irregular curved line, lending itself to attractive, flowing designs of infinite variety.

Do not attempt to fill all the areas of any line plan, instead use portions of open space to create a contrast against the decorated areas. If you feel that a particular area does need a small amount of decoration, but nothing too elaborate, then consider the use of plain bulbs or dots piped in the same medium used for coating the cake, such as fondant, buttercream or chocolate. This is a discreet way of adding decoration and is really only noticed and emphasised by the shadow created on, and adjacent to the bulb itself. Many of the designs in the book include these bulbs, often in graduated sizes.

Basic design.

A more balanced appearance achieved by using base coating colour bulbs.

Piped border and run-sugar collar designs are dealt with in the following chapters, However, the more basic, piped borders will be used on gateaux, layer cake and torten, and it is on these smaller type units that equal consideration should be given to proportion, that is proportion of the top and side decoration. If the top decoration is very elaborate then keep the borders reasonably simple, even omit the top border and simply decorate the base. When the two borders are used always keep the top one slightly smaller than the base border otherwise a 'top heavy', unbalanced effect will result, this is illustrated with run out design on page 124.

To fully compliment the overall appearance of the cake, side decoration should also be given careful thought. A shallow sided cake such as a sandwich type gateaux or torte, with a border may not require any decoration whatsoever on the sides. While a less elaborate design may benefit from a side decoration which creates a contrast in colour or texture with the top. Examples of side decoration are shown on page 83.

The following pages showing figs. 38 to 44 illustrate in step-by-step form the construction of cake designs, each starting with a basic line plan. The motifs and decorations are briefly described and are intended as guidelines only. However, it is up to you the creative confectioner to eventually use your own discretion and design ability to alter and adapt the colour and flavour combinations, materials and techniques used to suit your own requirements.

Please Note

When referring to linework, and lettering in the descriptions which accompany the following designs, the word CHOCOLATE usually describes chocolate coloured (and flavoured if desired) Royal Icing or Fondant or Piping Chocolate.

FIG. 37. Layout lines for gateaux and layer cakes

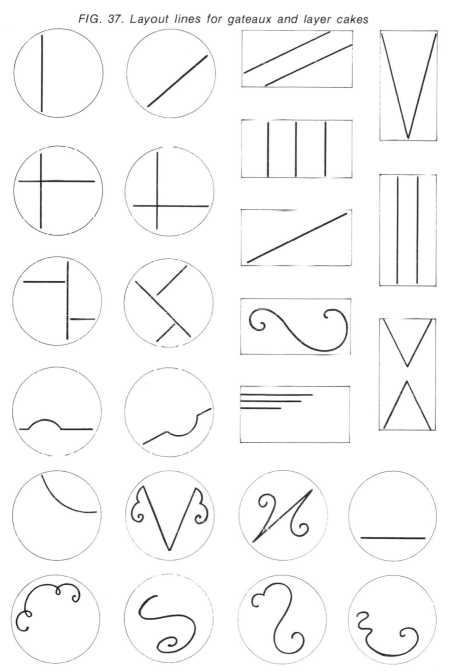

FIG. 38

Constructing a design using the single line layout basis. In this case a thick buttercream line is used. Using the same basic line, many designs can be created by varying the other decoration. Here we have changed the cut marzipan 'Guy Fawkes' for Father Christmas and a floral arrangement.

A. Pale peach colour fondant or buttercream base with a white buttercream line.

B. Low-relief marzipan cut-out of 'Guy Fawkes' and a white sugarpaste plaque with directly piped chocolate coloured lettering.

C. Piped blue curved linework.

D. Two yellow, white or orange sugarpaste stars used instead of the previously mentioned bulbs, these help carry through the Nov. 5th theme and yet still help to balance the design.

E. White fondant base, coffee coloured buttercream line. Red and white low-relief marzipan cut-out of Father Christmas. Directly piped chocolate lettering, white snowflakes and two silver dragees.

F. Lemon coloured fondant base, coffee coloured buttercream line with chocolate wavy line. A white sugarpaste flower with an orange centre, green piped stems and an outline of green royal icing or fondant filled in with greengage piping jelly to form the leaves. Graduated bright orange bulbs on lower stem.

FIG. 39

A wider single line than used in the previous examples forms the basis of the designs on page 50, the line could be rib-rolled marzipan or sugarpaste or even replaced with an outline of chocolate to be filled in with a coloured piping jelly.

A. Lemon coloured fondant with coffee coloured rib-rolled marzipan strip.

B. Low-relief cut-out yellow marzipan chick motif is positioned alongside line.

C. Green wavy line in royal icing or fondant, piped with a number 1 tube. Directly piped lettering in chocolate icing or fondant.

D. Three base colours fondant bulbs added to balance and complete the design.

E. Coffee coloured buttercream base, with cocoa powder dredged stencil shape. Rib-rolled coffee marzipan strip overpiped with wavy chocolate line. Three bulbs of buttercream with a half walnut on each. White sugarpaste inscription plaque with directly piped lettering.Three small bulbs complete the design.

F. Pale pink fondant base, pink rib-rolled sugarpaste strip with thick white buttercream line. Red or chocolate marzipan heart, curved line in chocolate fondant or royal icing with silver dragees in between. Directly piped lettering in deep pink and three base coloured bulbs.

FIG. 38

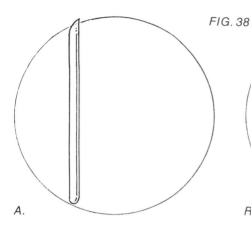

A.

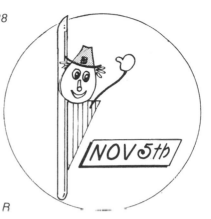

B.

C.

D.

E.

F.

FIG. 39

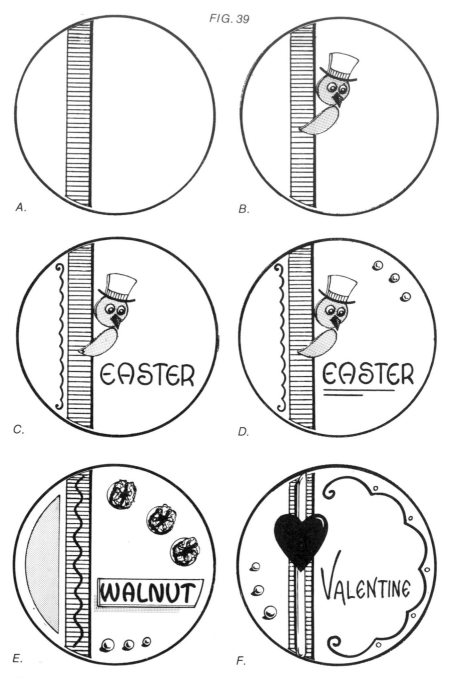

A.

B.

C.

D.

E.

F.

FIG. 40

A variation on a single line plan with the line positioned at an angle.

A. Pale orange fondant with a chocolate outline strip filled in with orange piping jelly.

B. Milk chocolate cut-out semi-circle pieces for the flower petals. Green, curved royal icing piped lines and five silver dragees. A fine chocolate curved line complete the design.

C. Pale pink fondant with chocolate strip. Note the use of a stencil for the cherry motif in red and green. Pre-fabricated sugarpaste lettering blocks form the inscription (see Chapter 10 - Lettering). Base coloured fondant bulbs complete the decoration.

D. Lemon coloured buttercream with a pale green rib-rolled marzipan strip and a fine chocolate line. Lilac coloured sugar flower and green leaves. White sugarpaste inscription plaque with directly piped chocolate lettering and base coloured bulbs complete the design.

E. Lemon fondant with a strip outlined in chocolate fondant and filled in with lemon curd. Directly piped lettering with illuminated capital. Lemon buttercream rosette with lemon jelly slice and a touch of green nibs. Chocolate linework and base coloured bulbs.

F. Pale pink fondant, pink sugarpast strip. Lilac coloured sugarpaste flower, green leaf and curved line. Directly piped chocolate coloured lettering Three parallel pink lines and two silver dragees.

FIG 41

Shown on page 53 are designs based on two angled lines used together still achieving the single line type layout basis.

A. Pale green fondant with two coffee coloured buttercream lines and a scalloped chocolate line.

B. Lilac coloured flower with green leaves.

C. Deeper lilac coloured directly piped lettering.

D. Base coloured bulbs.

E. Pale lemon coloured fondant with two white buttercream lines. Low-relief coffee coloured cut-out of rabbit on a light green base. Directly piped chocolate coloured lettering and linework. Five small base coloured bulbs.

F. White or pale pink coloured fondant base with pink or coffee coloured buttercream lines and a chocolate wavy line. Three red sugarpaste hearts half dipped in chocolate and a white sugarpaste inscription plaque- choc lettering. Two silver dragees and three base coloured bulbs.

FIG. 40

A.

B.

C.

D.

E.

F.

FIG. 41

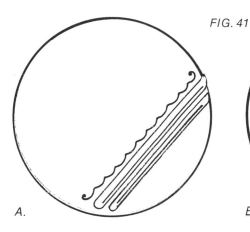

A.

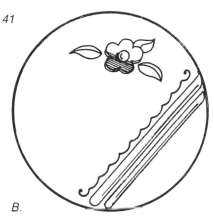

B.

C.

D.

E.

F.

FIG. 42

The two line layout, using thick buttercream lines. It can be seen from the illustrations opposite how easy it is to create several variations on the same layout simply by changing the motif and lettering.

A. Pale pink fondant, white buttercream lines.

B. Lilac or pink coloured sugar flower and green leaves.

C. Deeper pink or lilac curved scratch lines. Directly piped chocolate coloured lettering.

D. Base coloured bulbs.

E. Pale orange fondant base, white buttercream lines, small white bulbs, for balance and to depict 'snow' theme. Chocolate linework and red lettering. Orange marzipan bells with green holly and red berries.

F. Pale pink buttercream base - white buttercream lines. Jelly or marzipan strawberry. Chocolate wavy lines and white inscription plaque with choc lettering, white or base coloured bulbs.

FIG. 43

Two line designs using combinations of cut chocolate, marzipan or sugarpaste strips with thick buttercream lines.

A. Pale pink fondant base, coffee coloured sugarpaste strip and white buttercream line.

B. White buttercream line overpiped with chocolate wavy line. Straight line piped in chocolate. Two pink or lilac sugarpaste flowers.

C. Green sugarpaste or royal icing leaves. Directly piped chocolate lettering.

D. Green curved lines and base coloured bulbs.

E. Coffee coloured buttercream base. Chocolate strip and chocolate line. Three rosettes of buttercream with a whole hazelnut on each. Prepared sugarpaste inscription plaque and base coloured bulbs.

F. Pale green fondant base, pale green sugarpaste strip. White buttercream line, and thin chocolate line. Piped chocolate 'Fir Tree' type branches positioned at an angle off the cake. Green holly, red berries, white dots of silver dragees and a white curved line. Deep coffee coloured stenciled inscription.

FIG. 42

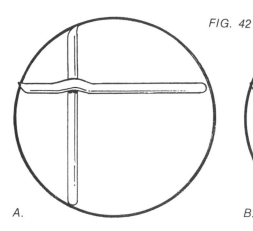

A.

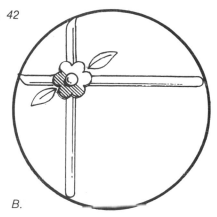

B.

C.

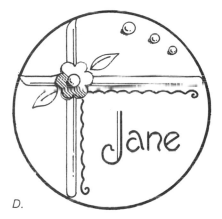

D.

E.

F.

FIG. 43

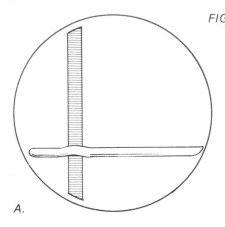

A.

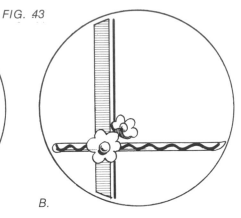

B.

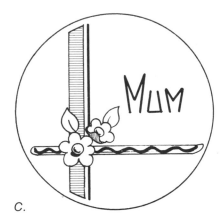

C.

D.

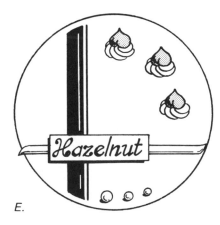

E.

F.

FIG. 44

When constructing designs based on irregular curved lines it is usually easier to start with the required motif and form the curved line around it, as opposed to the previous layouts where the lines are positioned first.

A. Plain chocolate base,, used here to help depict a night sky and bonfire type theme. The 'Catherine wheel' motif is a half-relief marzipan or sugarpaste model in white with blue bands and 'touch paper' and a chocolate drop centre.

B. The curved line is started by following the motif shape in blue royal icing (or better still A 50/50 mixture of royal icing and fondant to assist adhesion to the chocolate surface) piped in a number 2 tube.

C. Irregular curved line completed.

D. Directly piped bright orange lettering is added.

E. Two cut-out sugarpaste stars in white or yellow are positioned. These stars have replaced the base coloured bulbs we have been using on previous designs, we are still using them to help balance the design, whilst at the same time carrying through the November 5th theme.

F. White bulbs complete the design, stars on both sides would make the design a little 'fussy' and overcrowded.

Note:

Irregular curved line designs can be made easier to draw and pipe using the template method described in fig. 34. (page 43).

BALANCE, SPACING AND LAYOUT

Being confronted with individual designs for lettering, motif and maybe a numeral to be arranged within an allocated space and shape of a cake top, can be a daunting task, until one acquires a more experienced eye for balance and spacing. A simple method can be employed to ease the situation. First make individual tracings of the already prepared designs for lettering, motifs, which may be a marzipan cut-out, painted plaque or run-sugar figure etc., and if used a numeral for the age or anniversary etc., which again depending on the type of cake could be cut-marzipan, directly piped or a run-sugar 21 etc. Cut the tracings to separate them, and then using an outline shape the same size as the cake to be decorated arrange the tracings in various layouts, moving them around until the most pleasing effect of balance and spacing is achieved.

This techique can be carried out directly on the cake top, however it may be necessary sometimes to reverse a figure or motif image, obviously this would be more practical carried out at the initial design stages. When positioning cake top decoration, always take into consideration the space required for piped borders, run-out collars and linework.

Once you are satisfied with the overall appearance, lightly secure the tracings with a small piece of masking tape and make a full tracing of the complete design. In the case of positioning directly onto cake tops, scratch the tracing onto the surface with a fine needle or compass point, fig. 50.

FIG: 44

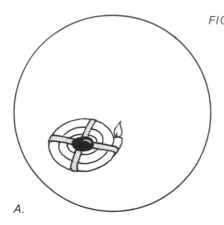

A.

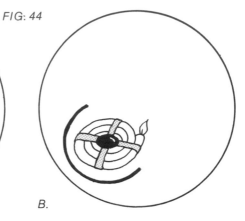

B.

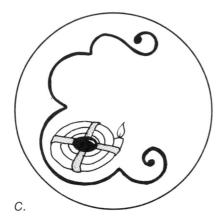

C.

D.

E.

F.

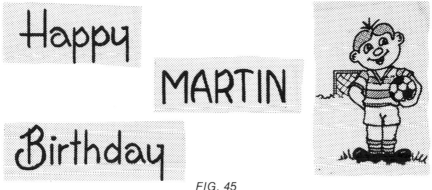

FIG. 45

Prepare tracings of each item of decoration, shown here as inscription and painted figure.

FIG. 46

Place the tracings onto the design and re-arrange them until a pleasing, balanced effect is achieved. Then trace into position.

FIG. 47

An alternative arrangement is used here. The position of the head having been altered. Note also that the eyes have been directed at the lettering.

FIG. 48

Still using the same tracings, yet another arrangement is obtained. Note the use of a line to link 'Happy' and 'Birthday' together.

FIG. 49

Arrangement on a square cake top.

59

This tracing may be used for all celebration cakes, gateaux, torten and fancies etc., to experiment with the positioning of cream rosettes, fruit, piped chocolate pieces, in fact any form of decoration to be used. You could even prepare and keep cut-outs of good quality tracings of popular decorative items such as the one just mentioned, to be used as a form of "jigsaw" for confectionery design.

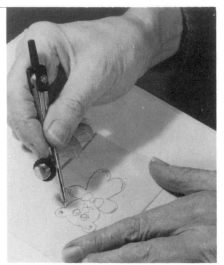

FIG. 50
Using a compass point to 'dot' motif outline onto a royal iced surface. (Tracing, pencil side uppermost).

FIG. 51
Tracings for design layout of a royal iced Birthday Cake.

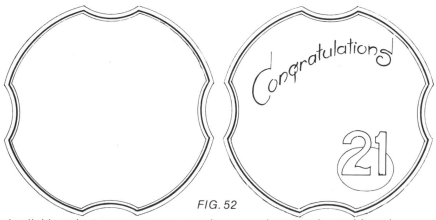

FIG. 52

Available cake top area, represented by the linework outline of a cake top.

Incorrectly positioned. Inscription too high, motif too low. Both are too near linework and edge of cake.

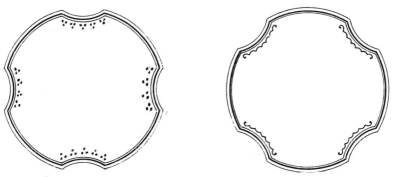

Dot formation.   *FIG. 53*   Scratched line.

When spacing and balancing inscriptions and motifs on cake tops, take into consideration any possible decoration extra to the linework such as dot formations and scratched lines, which further reduce available space.

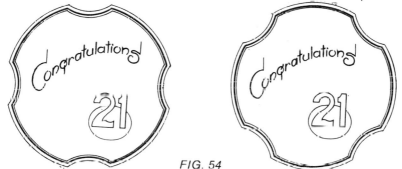

FIG. 54

Two pleasing layouts using the same inscription and motif in almost the same positions, however, slight variations have been made to accommodate the TWO different positions of the linework curves.

FIG. 55

Lettering and motif sizes too large for allocated area, letters 'C' and 'S' are too near, and almost touching the linework.

Here another pleasing layout is achieved using a simple horizontal plane for both lettering and motif.

FIG. 56

Experiment with your layouts, many interesting and pleasing effects can be produced. Above we can see variations of the same basic design theme all using; INSCRIPTION, 21st MOTIF, and FLORAL ARRANGEMENT to create six different layouts.

Here are some points worth remembering when arranging decoration on cake tops. If a 'scene' type of design is being used featuring a 'ground level', then appropriately position this at the base of the cake top area with the lettering in the 'sky' position, so as not to create the impression that the ground is 'floating in mid-air'.

FIG. 57

For a 'life-like' scene effect, position 'land' or 'water' at the base and lettering in the 'sky' position.

Children's cakes allow for a little imagination and 'make-belief'.

Likewise if say for instance balloons or a kite is to be part of the design, make them appear to be floating in air at the top of the design area. Both the above points are common sense, however they are often mis-used thus resulting in unrealistic arrangements. I suppose the exception to this would be in the case of a cartoon type design dominated by 'make belief'.

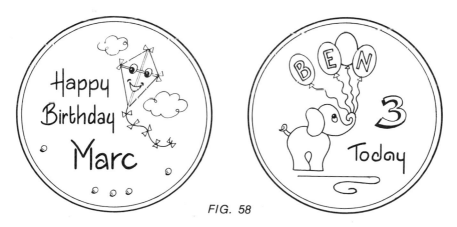

FIG. 58

Figures or animal motifs, in most situations look a more integral part of the arrangement when they are seen to be looking into the layout and not off the cake (except in certain instances when the expression doesn't allow for this). Try to direct the eyes of the figure or animal, or even point an arm or finger of the figure at the name, age or an important part of the inscription within the layout.

FIG. 59

In all arrangements ensure that a pleasing continuity exists within the layout of the design, so that the main part such as the name Alan stands out followed by probably a greeting; It's your 5th Birthday with the numeral emphasized as much as the name, these being the most important points of the message. The figure, animal or main subject of a scene should compliment the overall inscription so that one does not compete against the other to be noticed. Any background or other less obvious decoration or detail should compliment and add to the completeness of the arrangement as a whole.

FIG. 60

REDUCTION AND ENLARGEMENT OF DRAWINGS

From time to time you will no doubt require motifs produced from edible materials to decorate cakes for special occasions, these can be in the form of low-relief marzipan models, run-out figures, painted plaques, directly painted cake tops or even figures or scenes reproduced in chocolate and various piping jellies. These various types of decoration can be seen on cake designs throughout this book. In many cases the picture is either too large or too small to fit the area of space allocated on the cake top, and unless you have access to a pantograph or one of the modern photo-copy machines with reduction and enlargement facilities which reproduce a drawing of the correct size, copying and reducing or enlarging at the same time by hand can sometimes prove difficult.

A reasonably simple method of altering the size of a drawing and still keeping it in proportion is to first of all draw in pencil a grid of squares over the design to be altered, fig. 61, the average sized greeting card could be divided into 3/4" squares. Another grid is then drawn on a separate sheet of paper with larger or smaller squares depending on the alteration required, these would be calculated as near as possible to fractions of the original drawing squares; for example fig. 61b drawing has been enlarged by 1/3rd therefore 1" were used.
fig. 61c shows a drawing reduced to 2/3rd the size of the original picture therefore 1/2" squares were used.

As can be seen from the illustrations the squares on the original picture and the squares for the alteration drawing are numbered and lettered in the same place for easy reference during the copying process. All that is required is to carefully follow the outlines from the original and copy them onto the prepared grid. Using the squares as guidelines one can copy for example the end of the elephants trunk and bottom of the ear from square number 4C and so on until the picture is completed.

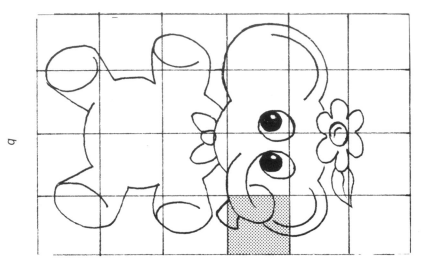

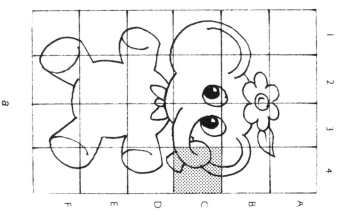

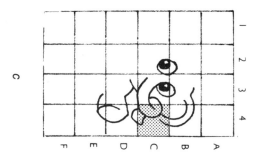

FIG. 61

66

CHAPTER 7

Textures and Cakes Sides

CREAM AND ICING TEXTURES

Texture plays an important part in the techniques used to apply various decorative mediums. The textures produced by a confectioner more often than not will rely on shadows cast from the varying degrees in height, shape, and form of different raised surfaces to reveal a regular pattern. One must not forget texture when designing confectionery products, the initial appearance of a product can be made far more interesting by the use of textures, in a similar way that the eating qualities of food can be improved by the combination of different textures, i.e. soft custards and creams, the firmer marzipans and pastes along with crunchy brittle nuts or croquant, all have characteristics of their own and when combined in different ways, provide interest to a product. This kind of texture is experienced through eating the product whereas the designer is concerned more with visual texture, however one is rarely never considered without the other, as an uninteresting end product may result with flavours, consistencies and textural materials that do not compliment each other sufficiently.

Textures can be supplied through several of the commonly used decorative materials; creams, icings, pastes chocolate etc. The easiest way to commence experimenting and practicing with texture related to cream and icing finishes is to use a well beaten mixture consisting of equal quantities of fat (white shortening) and sieved flour, because this mixture will not readily 'crust' or 'skin' over it becomes an ideal medium to continually reapply to cake dummies without rapid deterioration. Also very useful for piping and cake coating practice.

Here are some ideas to try.

FIG 62

Many variations can be made from this one idea of paddling the material with the tip of a pallete knife, try overlapping in different ways.

FIG. 63

A smooth surface (obtained with a straight edge) is marked with the blunt side of a long knife. Various patterns can be formed with this method. In practice a coloured butter or filling cream lightly dredged with icing sugar and then marked in a diamond pattern as shown produces an attractive finish.

FIG. 62

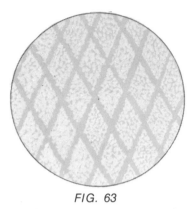

FIG. 63

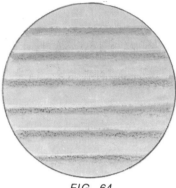

FIG. 64

FIG. 64

Straight lines produced with the tip of a pallete knife drawn across the coated surface.

FIG. 65

Shows how the basic pattern in fig. 64 can be made more interesting by drawing a pointed knife over the surface to produce pattern similar to a 'Marbling' technique.

FIG. 66

Lines are radiated out from one point, in this case at the base of the design.

FIG. 67

Lines are pulled out in opposite directions.

FIG. 68

Coat the surface, then pull the palette knife tip outwards from the centre of the cake, out to the edge whilst rotating the turntable at the same time.

FIG. 69

A stage further from fig. 68, lines have been pulled out from the centre to give a spiral, spiders web, or log-end effect.

Other interesting textures can be obtained by 'peaking' the surface with the tip of the pallete knife or by 'stippling' with a small piece of foam sponge.

FIG. 65

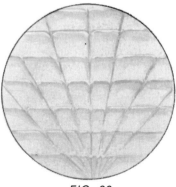

FIG. 66

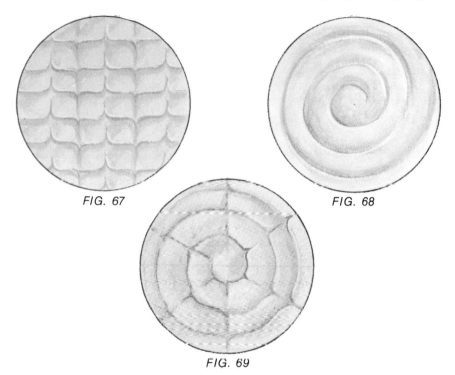

FIG. 67   FIG. 68

FIG. 69

MARZIPAN AND SUGARPASTE TEXTURES

All of the textures described previously are ideal to use when decorating with butter or filling creams, many commercial gateaux are seen to be quickly finished in this way, and in many cases this is the only decoration given. Nevertheless more elaborate finishes can be achieved when textures used are in conjunction with other forms of decoration and materials.

Marzipan and sugarpastes lend themselves ideally to surface texture treatment. One point I consider to be very important when using these materials is the final appearance of the surface. After rolling, always ensure to 'polish' the surface, rotate the clean, sugar-free palm of your hand over the paste with a little pressure to remove excess icing sugar and leave a clean, bright colour, instead of the too often seen dull, powdery finish on this type of material.

Roll out the paste in the usual manner, polish the surface, and then with the aid of various patterned rollers, which can be obtained from bakery equipment manufacturers we can produce interesting textures as shown in fig. 70.

FIG. 70a

Ribbed roller to produce parallel lines. Note the use of half a roller patterned surface to allow for a motif or inscription.

69

FIG. 70b

Boxwood roller pattern. To produce a similar effect use a ribbed roller twice, with the second roll at right angles to the first.

FIG. 70c

Ribbed rolling at an angle.

FIG. 70d

Use of a basket weave roller.

FIG. 70e

A rolling pin wrapped with plastic coated electrical flex is used here to produce a quite useful effect suitable for novelty cake roofs and fences, and also to produce a realistic 'bark' effect for the manufacture of chocolate yule logs.

FIG. 70f

Rolling pins with a plastic based household filler piped on through a number 2 tube can be used to produce some very interesting effects, such as brickwork, stone and tortoise shell.

Even more effect can be given to an already textured surface by using the aerograph to spray colour and emphasize the raised surfaces. This method of applying colour is especially useful for brickwork and the bark of chocolate yule logs.

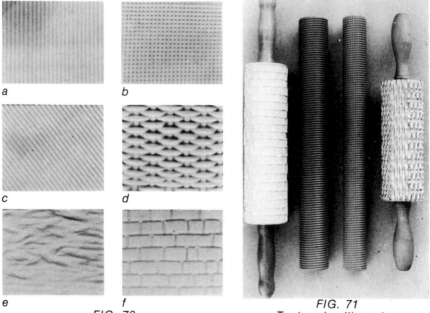

FIG. 70.
Texture effects on Marzipan
and Sugarpaste.

FIG. 71
Textured rolling pins.
Left to right: Brickwork, Ribbed,
Boxwood and Basketweave.

CAKES SIDES

When planning your celebration cake and gateaux designs, side decoration should be given equally as much thought and consideration as the cake top, and in the case of royal iced cakes, the cake board decoration. If anything should be slightly more noticeable on single tiered cakes then it should be the top decoration carrying the greeting, name and motif, but as a general rule side and top decoration should compliment each other, remembering that the side should not compete against the top to be noticed.

Tiered wedding cakes are generally viewed by guests at a reception more from the side than the top, the top being partially hidden from view and more difficult to see without very close inspection, decoration therefore would be concentrated more on the sides. Royal iced cakes allow for the more fine, intricate type of decoration associated with the characteristic longer drying period of this medium. Different manufacturing techniques also enable several forms of prefabricated decoration to be produced. In complete contrast the type of materials used to finish gateaux and layer cake such as creams, fondants and preserves coupled with their shorter shelf life, we rely on a quicker somewhat simpler side decoration mainly in the form of textures provided by jap crumb, vermicelli and various nut maskings, also the numerous variety of cut marzipan, sugarpaste and chocolate pieces and piped chocolate shapes.

Gateaux and layer cakes sides are shown on page 83.

The simplest of all royal iced cake sides must be the basic two or three coats of icing with the final coat being carried out using a conventional straight side scraper fig. 72. Executed correctly this finish with further simple decoration is quite acceptable, in fact cake sides of this nature, with reasonably plain or simple finishes are usually widely favoured by many high class cake decorators, at least by the ones who can successfully coat a cake. The main reason is that the cake decorators skill is emphasised more by a neatly executed exposed coated surface as opposed to cake sides, the coated surfaces of which could be inferior, being heavily camouflaged with wide ribbon or cake band. This is not to say that ribbon or band should be omitted from your list of decorations, quite the contrary, used in moderation with thought given to colour, width and position on the cake, ribbon and band can be tastefully incorporated onto the cake side design, especially when used in conjunction with some of the following layouts.

The use of colour, stencils, spraying techniques and various cut scrapers, added to, or even replacing the conventional final coat of icing can produce attractive, eyecatching textures and effects. For many of the layouts shown there is little extra work involved, as the cake would still be receiving a final coat of icing.

The illustrations are intended to feature side designs, and should be used with discretion, according to the shape of the run-out collar or the form of the piped border being employed at the top and base of the cake. Try as far as possible to carry a theme throughout the whole design, for example the "scalloped' design in fig. 73 lends itself particularly well to the shape of a tapered rope border (page 95) whilst the side design in fig. 79 could be matched to a run-out collar of a similar shape to that in fig. 154.

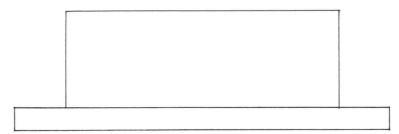

FIG. 72

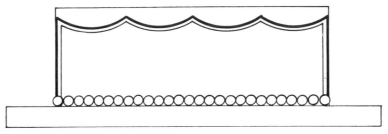

FIG. 73

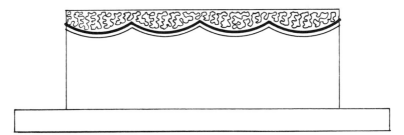

FIG. 74

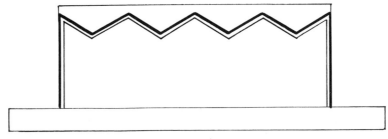

FIG. 75

Try various combinations of the following cake sides described, and include in them the use of piped decorations such as doves, bells, butterflies, cupids, flowers and figures etc., and complimentary dot and line designs.

Before experimenting with some of the not so commonly used ideas mentioned in this section, do not forget the more conventionally used piped side designs and panel ideas. These are actually built up with the 321 system of linework using combinations of tubes number 2 and number 1 or tubes number 3 and number 2. (See pages 90, 91).

Some of the shapes, such as half loops (scallop shapes) fig. 73 can be piped free-hand after marking the cake off into divisions, other more involved designs would require the aid of a paper template. It will be necessary to tilt the cake at an angle by resting it against a sturdy object or using a piece of equipment specifically made for that purpose. Tilting the cake allows the line to drop onto the cake in the right place without stretching or sagging as would probably happen if the cake was piped while at right angles.

FIG. 73
Scallop or half loop design. Number 2 and number 1, or number 3 and number 2 tubes.

FIG. 74
As for fig. 73, with a fine filigree design piped directly onto the cake using a number 1 or number 0 tube - could be coloured or base coloured.

FIG. 75
Angular type pattern, piped as for fig. 73.

FIG. 76
Using a paper template placed against the side of the cake, many attractive continuous line designs can be produced. Use the spaces to incorporate other decorative motifs.

FIG. 77
Again using templates, individual panels can be piped which in turn may be further decorated with flowers, monogram or butterfly etc.

FIG. 78
Three sided panel shapes, incorporating spaces for piped or moulded flowers or silver horseshoe.

FIG. 79
Here a template is used to mask off the lower part of the cake side, the top section panel shape is stippled or textured with royal icing using a small piece of foam sponge. After removing the template an edging line to follow the panel shape may be piped using tubes number 2 and number 1.

Shaped panels can be used in many ways to add decoration to cake sides, which in turn more often than not are used as backgrounds for piped monograms, animals, doves, butterflies and figures for such as wedgewood designs.

First cut a template from cartridge paper to cover the depth of the cake. Draw in the required panel shape of which there are several to choose from, round, square, oval, hexagonal, octagonal, pentagon and more decorative shapes such as heart and flower shapes also diamond, triangle, and lozenge

73

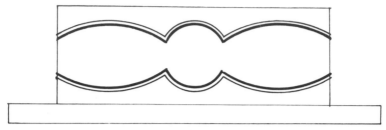

FIG. 76

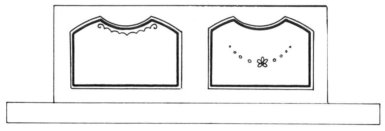

FIG. 77

FIG. 78

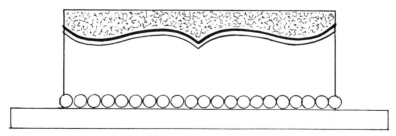

FIG. 79

shapes. When planning the panel design try to match it to the overall design of the cake, taking into account such factors as number of cake sides if decorating say an octagonal or other multi sided cake, divisions in piped or run-out border design to be used and of course the shape of the motif to be used in each panel to create a balanced effect without looking cramped or indeed lost.

FIG. 80

Cut out a heart shape from the paper template. Place the template to the cake side. Then coat with royal icing, coloured icing shows up well on the white background of wedding cakes. Smooth the panel off with a palette knife, allow to crust over then remove the template.

With texture in mind once again, fig. 81 illustrates the use of a paper template with a central band removed, the band could be straight on one side and scalloped on the other as shown, or it could be edged with a wavy or angular line design. The template is secured to the cake and the sides are coated as normal, probably using a harmonious or contrasting colour of icing to that of the base colour. Whilst the royal icing is still 'wet' liberally dredge the sides with granulated or rock sugar (hot syrup with royal icing added). Remove the template to reveal a textured centre panel with two smooth outer surfaces. The smooth surfaces could be used for further decoration.

FIG. 82

A template with a panel cut-out similar to the idea in fig 80 is prepared, this time the cut-out is an oval shape. In this finish, instead of spreading the panel with royal icing a colour has been applied via the aerograph spray gun (see chapter 14). Ensure to 'mask off' all areas that are not to be sprayed to prevent colour mist settling on them.

FIG. 83

Colour spraying technique used to edge the top of the cake side with an angular line design. The sides are then finished with a build-up of piped linework following the sprayed pattern edge.

FIG. 84 and 85

Experiment with the 'spray and template' technique used previously to produce a side design with a pictorial theme, skyline of a city or other easily recognisable shapes and images such as the two Christmas cake designs shown. Many interesting effects can be achieved.

A similar effect is used to produce the stencil for the Halloween cake on page 270.

FIG. 86a

Here we see what is most probably the most widely used 'quick' finish for a celebration cake, the ever faithful satin ribbon and bow. As mentioned earlier used with care it does look quite presentable. fig. 86b shows a small spotted design suitable for a child's cake.

FIG. 87a.

Again another widely used decorative material, Silver and Gold cake band, available with many different embossed designs and in various widths.

FIG. 87b

Velvet ribbon, particularly useful when matching a colour scheme for a wedding cake, to the bridesmaids dress colour.

FIG. 80

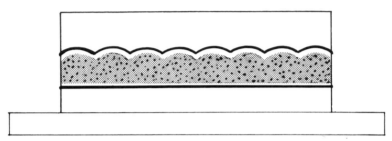

FIG. 81

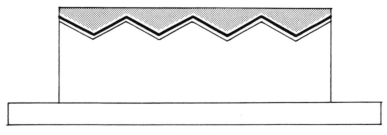

FIG. 82

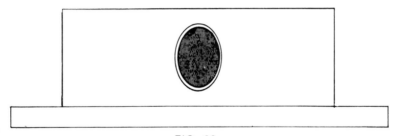

FIG. 83

FIG. 84

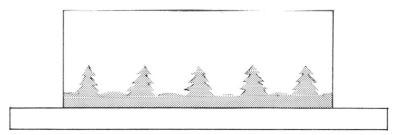

FIG. 85

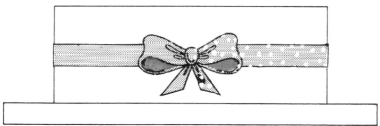

a   *FIG. 86*   b

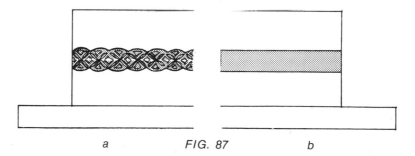

a   *FIG. 87*   b

FIG. 88

To give the impression of directly piped side linework as shown in figs. 89 to 92 the cake decorator can prepare various 'CUT SCRAPERS' made by removing small sections from a standard plastic scraper by:

Melting with a heated compass point;

or Filing with a small narrow file;

or Cutting 'V' shapes out with scissors.

Numerous interesting combinations of parallel lines round the cake sides can be designed, these can be placed centrally, off centre or grouped in varying sizes fig. 89 to create the impression of tiered linework piped using the 3, 2, 1 build up or variations on that theme. Further decoration can be introduced in the form of velvet ribbon, silver or gold band being placed on or against the line, or between two lines as shown in fig. 90.

The lines may also be used as guides to enable various curved line designs to be added fig. 91 shows two examples, a floral arrangement and a Christmas theme using a holly leaf and berry.

FIG. 92

Shows the use of a two line cut scraper to produce lines on the cake sides, onto which 'dropped' lines my be piped using a small plain tube to give a delicate 'open' base border design. Before piping the dropped lines, small pearl bulbs or tiny shells could first be piped in, perhaps in a different colour of icing.

Comb scraping fig. 93a is widely used as a means of decorating with dairy and filling creams, even chocolate. The effect is obtained with a comb or serrated scraper which are available from bakery sundriesmen and ingredient manufacturers. Comb scraping on royal iced cakes can be made more interesting by first coating the cake in deep coloured icing e.g. chocolate, the top could be coated in pink. When the sides are dry, coat over the deep colour with pink used for the top and comb scrape in the usual manner to reveal a light comb on a dark background fig. 93b Experiment also with the light and dark colours reversed. Wider lines of 'comb' can be made by cutting off the tips of the comb points.

FIG. 94

Using a single scraper we can produce a cake side with halt plain and half combed.

FIG. 95

Shows variation on the comb scrape theme with the centre cut-out to form a dome shape. Arrange this in the centre or towards the base, depending on the base border to be used. The dome shape at the top of the cake side could look a little top heavy if a delicate or narrow base border is to be used. This idea may be left as finished or the dome shape utilized as a background for further decoration.

For the finish shown in fig. 96 cut out a quarter circle from the base right angle corner of a plastic scraper. Apply the final coat of royal icing as usual with a palette knife, then pipe in, using a savoy tube of similar proportion to the cut out ring of royal icing around the cake base immediately take the cut out scraper around the cake as for conventional final coating. The resulting dome shape at the base of the cake can be decorated with various scallop and trellis designs as shown.

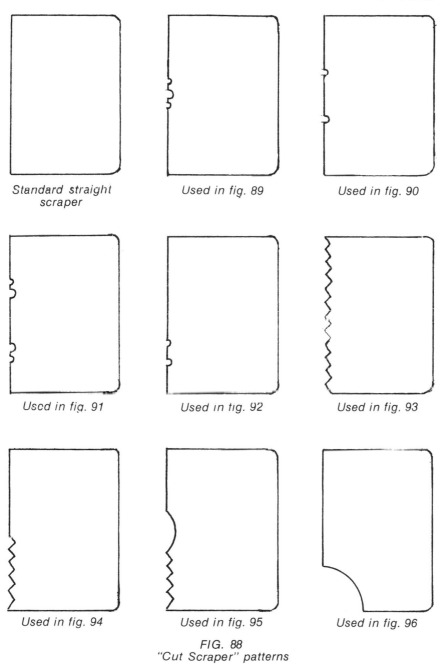

Standard straight
scraper

Used in fig. 89

Used in fig. 90

Used in fig. 91

Used in fig. 92

Used in fig. 93

Used in fig. 94

Used in fig. 95

Used in fig. 96

FIG. 88
"Cut Scraper" patterns

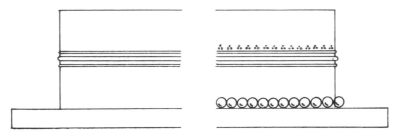

FIG. 89

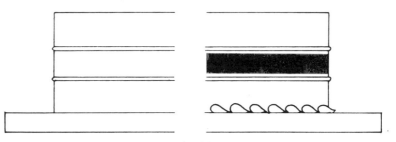

FIG. 90

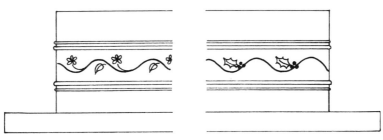

FIG. 91

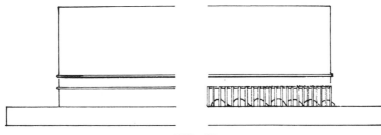

FIG. 92

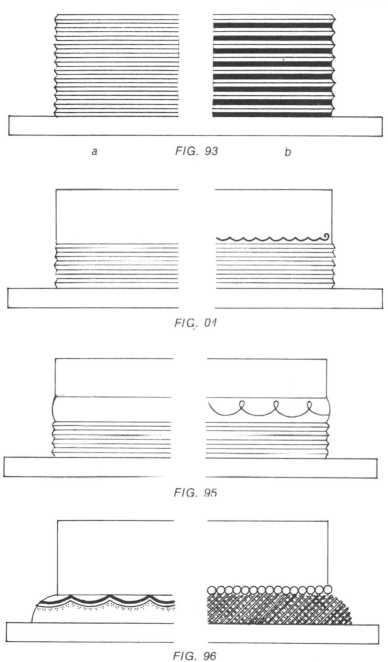

a   FIG. 93   b

FIG. 94

FIG. 95

FIG. 96

After all the time spent designing and applying the cake decoration, do not neglect the cake board as is so often seen, very little decoration is used on base boards. Use this area to create the illusion of a larger cake, to give it more 'weight' at the base and balance the overall effect and to give a sense of completeness to the finished product, extending the design out to the edge of the board from the cake sides.

Use 2, 3 or even more lines to build up a shape which compliments the piped border or run-out shape. An attractive finish for cakes decorated with run-outs as the top border is to cut a template the same shape as the run-out piece or use a spare $\frac{1}{4}$ run-out, place this on the coated base board, and outline with a plain tube, then remove the template (or run-out) and finish the build up of lines, perhaps completing the effect with a fine scratch line or dot design. Fill in the angle where the side meets the base with a small pearl, bulb or shell as shown below.

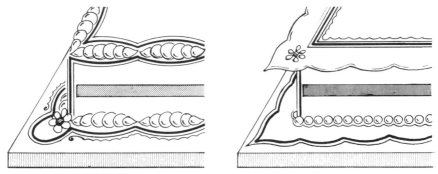

GATEAUX AND TORTE SIDE FINISHES. Fig. 97.

A. Roasted nibbed almonds.

B. Roasted flaked almonds.

C. Milk or plain chocolate vermicelli.

D. Milk or plain chocolate shavings.

E. Comb scraped dairy cream, buttercream or filling cream.

F. Cream masked sides, half masked with sieved jap crumbs and small cream bulbs to cover half-way edge.

G. Cut chocolate, cut marzipan or cut sugarpaste shapes positioned around base.

H. A variation of fig. G. Using different shapes also texturising effects, e.g. comb scraped chocolate or rib-rolled marzipan or sugarpaste.

I. Piped chocolate shapes positioned around base.

J. Small milk and plain chocolate drops or small cream bulbs arouna base. For a colourful childrens cake, coloured sweets could be used.

Note:
Figs. F, G, H, I, and J could be used to decorate cakes with cream masked sides or chocolate or fondant enrobed units.

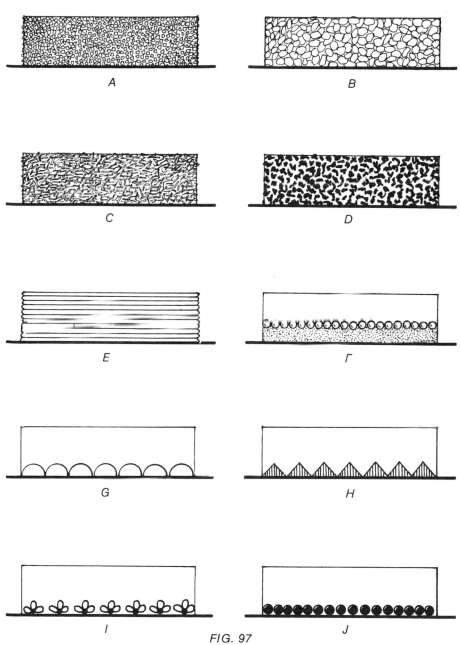

FIG. 97

Side maskings and decoration suitable for gateaux, torten and layer cake.

CHAPTER 8

Borders and Linework

The aim of this chapter is merely to provide examples of how to indicate piped borders and linework on a cake design. As mentioned in the introduction, the book is intended to be used by someone who has, or who is also studying the practical aspect of cake decoration, and therefore understands the various terms used to describe types of borders. Consequently they will have produced or at least seen this type of decoration. It only remains therefore to be able to draw and indicate borders on a design.

There are numerous types of borders, each with many permutations of overpiping. I have included the basic bulb, shell, ropes and scrolls with a few overpiping examples to show how to represent borders on a plan and side elevation drawing, enabling one to prepare a design and view the prospective idea before attempting to reproduce it in practice from raw materials. Illustrations showing how to indicate linework on a design are also included.

Having now progressed through the first chapters of the book which explain how to construct basic plan and side elevations, balance and space motifs, use textures, and design cake sides we can now add piped borders (also run-out collars chapter 9) and linework to produce a complete design. The design on page 44a features many of the previously mentioned design elements, along with the use of colour and a written specification to produce a complete design.

BORDERS

When designing and drawing your borders, remember to use the tracing and template techniques described on pages 40 and 42.

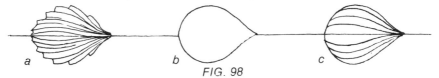

FIG. 98

a. Detailed drawing of a basic shell, piped using a star tube.

b. Basic shell shape piped using a plain tube.

c. Simplified drawing of a star piped shell, more suited for our design drawing purposes.

FIG. 99 Cream rosette shape.

'S' Scroll.

c

b

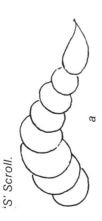

a

'C' Scroll.

c

b

a

Tapered rope.

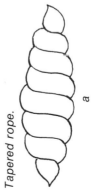

c

b

a

FIG. 100

a. *Piped using a plain tube number 3 or number 4.*

b. *Piped using a 44 star tube.*

c. *With overpiping.*

85

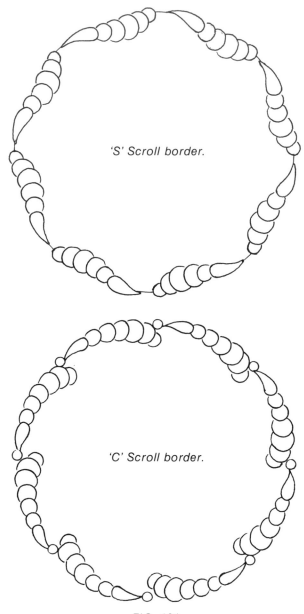

'S' Scroll border.

'C' Scroll border.

FIG. 101

Plan views of round celebration cakes showing a completed piped 'S' scroll
border and piped 'C' scroll border from fig. 100.

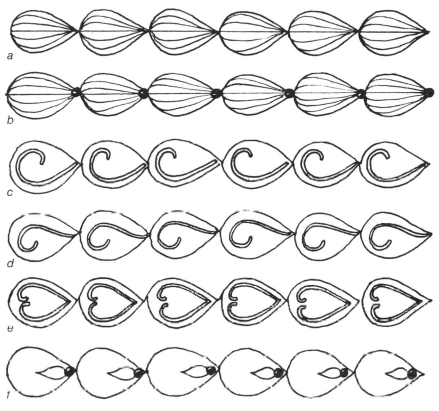

FIG. 102

PIPED SHELL BORDERS

a. Basic piped shell, using number 11, 12 or 13 star tube. Use number 7 or number 44 for smaller shells.

b. Basic piped shell with simple coloured dot finish, piped with a number 2 or number 1 tube.

c. Basic piped shell with 'C' shaped overpiping uning number 2 followod by a number 1*.

d. As for fig. c - reversed.

e. Basic shell with heart shaped overpiping design using number 2 then number 1 tube*.

f. Basic shell with piped leaf (green) and dot (red). Useful for a Christmas cake design to represent holly and berry.

To avoid confusion with too many lines, figs. c, d, e and f are shown as plain shells.

* Number 1 tube could be coloured.

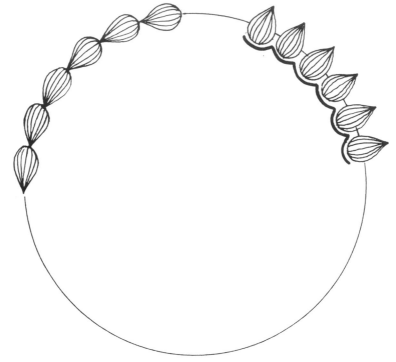

FIG. 103

*Plan view showing: left - conventionally piped shell border.
right - an interesting way of piping shells - radiating from the centre.*

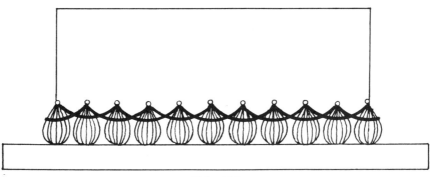

FIG. 104

Side elevation featuring shells piped upright, with a loop line design and tiny bulbs. This border looks very effective as a top edge border.

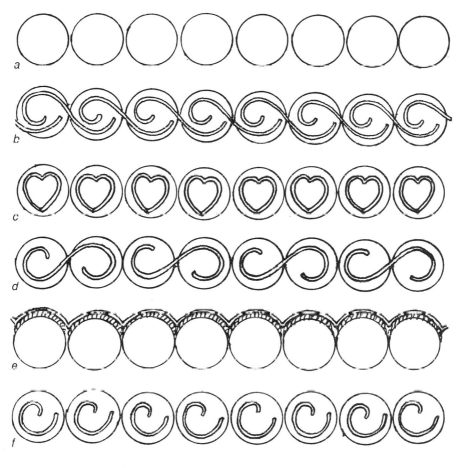

FIG. 105

PIPED BULB BORDERS

a. Basic piped bulb using number 3 or number 4 tube.

b. Basic piped bulb with reversed 'S' shaped overpiping.

c. Basic piped bulb with heart shaped overpiping, using number 2 tube followed by a number 1 tube.

d. Basic piped bulb with figure 8 shaped overpiping using tubes as for fig. c.

e. Basic piped bulb with fine rope edging piped using a number 2 tube, followed by further overpiping using a number 1 tube.

f. Basic piped bulb with 'c' shaped overpiping again using tubes number 2 and number 1.

Icing used to overpipe in number 1 tube could be coloured.

LINEWORK

Linework piping in royal icing, fondant or piping chocolate can be illustrated on a design simply by drawing lines of the required shape, of varying thickness to indicate the size of piping tube to be used, and also the appropriate colour to represent the icing or other piping medium. Coloured felt tip pens for complete designs and black felt tip pens for line drawings are ideal for this purpose, as are coloured pencil crayons. When drawing linework, do not try to draw freehand, straight or even curved lines. Use a ruler for the straight lines and a compass fitted with an adaptor to hold a felt tip pen (shown on page 5). For irregular curved lines use the template technique described on page 40.

Royal icing linework is often piped tiered, in various formations. This tiered linework or 'build-up' of lines can be referred to as 3,2,1 linework because of the three lines piped on top of each other, then two lines piped on top of each other and finally a single line all piped next to each other to merge or 'blend' a piped border or run-out collar with an iced surface on the top or side of a cake. The spacing of lines piped together in such groups is governed by, and usually the same width as the tubes being used to pipe the lines.

Tiered linework would be shown on a design as a series of varying thicknesses of lines as in figs. 106 to 109, however in the design specification a small line drawing of a cross-section of the linework could be included as in fig 110 to give details of the sizes of piping tubes used in the tiered formation.

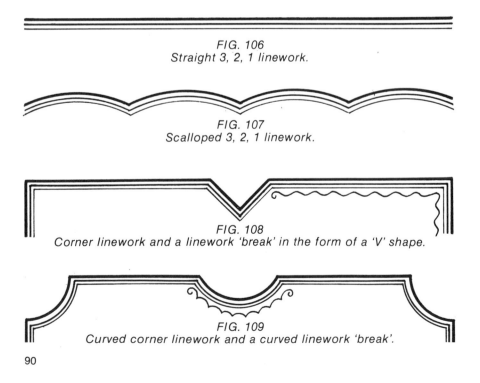

FIG. 106
Straight 3, 2, 1 linework.

FIG. 107
Scalloped 3, 2, 1 linework.

FIG. 108
Corner linework and a linework 'break' in the form of a 'V' shape.

FIG. 109
Curved corner linework and a curved linework 'break'.

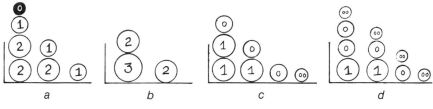

FIG. 110
Four examples of tiered linework.

a. Probably the most widely used formation, three sets of lines using in total six lines with a possible seventh in the form of a coloured line in a number 0 tube. If the number 0 tube is omitted, the number 1 topping the highest set of lines could be coloured if required.

b. A simpler application, using thicker tubes and less lines to enable quicker cake finishing with reduced detail and a heavier appearance.

c, Using four sets of lines, sometimes extended to five sets or even more, this
&   type of formation is used extensively in competition work. As you can see
d. from the drawings the decorator would use tubes number 0, 00, and 000 to achieve the required fineness and delicateness.

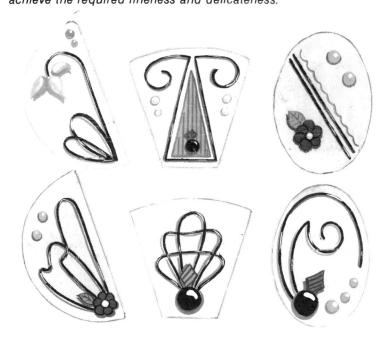

Linework is not restricted to large celebration cakes only, it is also extensively used as a form of decoration for smaller units such as fondant fancies shown here.

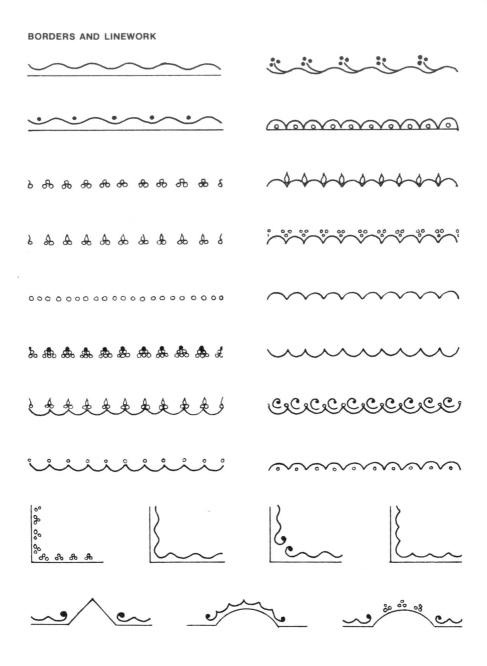

FIG. 111
A selection of directly piped scratched lines, dot formations and line designs,
for use alongside linework or as edgings for run-out collars, plaques etc.

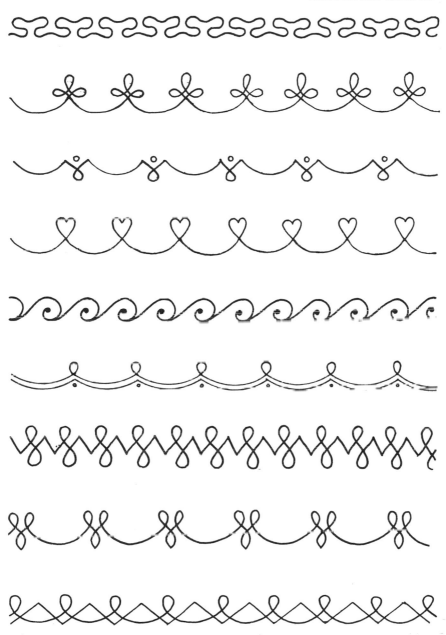

FIG. 112
A selection of useful piped line designs.

FIG. 113
A selection of useful piped line designs.

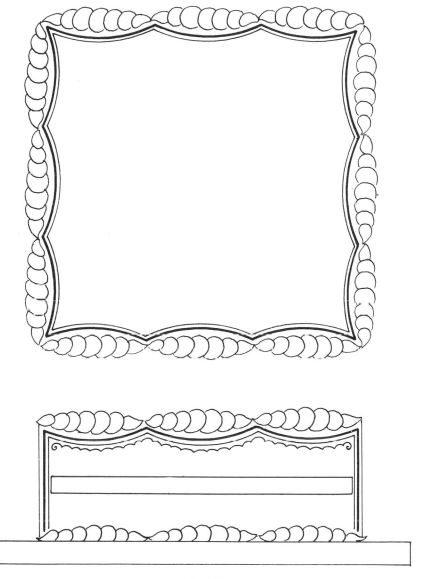

FIG. 114

Plan and side elevation for a square celebration cakes featuring top and base borders of piped tapered ropes. Inside top edge is finished with a set of two piped lines e.g. number 2 overpiped with coloured number 1, another number 1 base coloured line is piped alongside. Same linework is used on cake sides along with a scratched line.

95

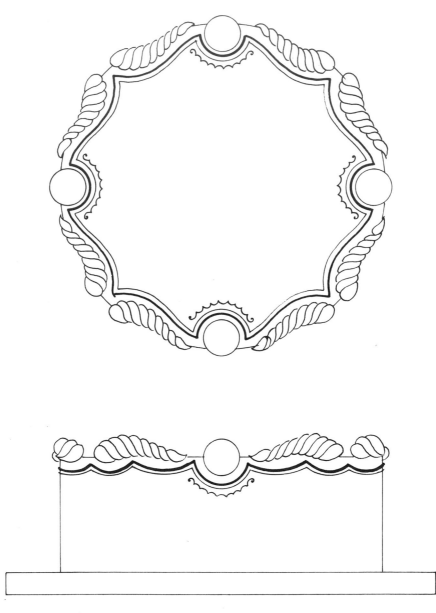

FIG. 115

Plan and side elevation for a round celebration cake featuring a top border of piped 'S' scrolls and reversed 'S' scolls, with piped bulbs to divide into four. Set of two lines piped around inside edge and cake sides as for fig. 114.

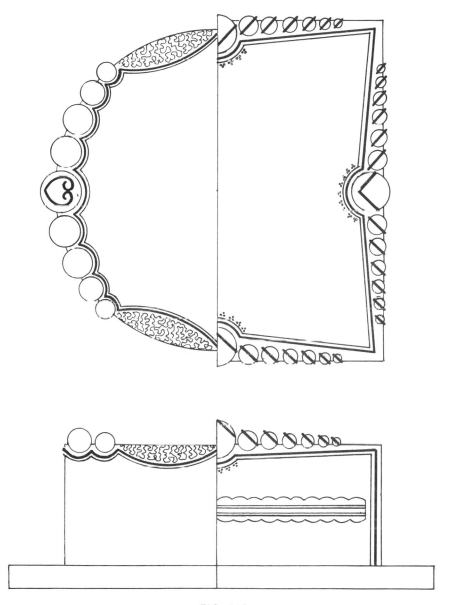

FIG. 116

Plan and side elevations of round and square celebration cakes, to illustrate how to indicate bulbs with and without overpiping, and directly piped filigree work.

97

CHAPTER 9

Run-out Design

Run sugar collars have become more and more popular over the past few years as a form of decoration for iced celebration cakes. They can be prepared somewhat in advance to the required date, and provide a cake with a neat, clean, precise and modern appearance.

I don't intend to give technical data as to the complete production techniques used in their manufacture, however, with the comprehensive collation of design techniques, ideas and illustrations within this chapter, one should be able to combine with it their own practical tuition and experience, fully understanding the characteristics and limitations of this form of decoration to produce successful and pleasing designs.

Run sugar collars can be defined as pre-fabricated units of dried royal icing, made on the 'run-out work' principle of outlining a given shape with royal icing via a fine piping tube normally onto waxed paper, filling in this outline with an albumen or water softened royal icing, again via a small aperture in a greaseproof piping bag, then drying in a very gentle heat to produce a smooth semi-glossy surfaced dried unit which can be peeled from it's waxed paper backing and attached to a cake with royal icing. Collars are used to decorate both the top edge and the base board of an iced celebration cake, the top collar protruding over the edge of the cake, in effect making the cake appear larger than it really is. Once assembled on the cake, the cake top surface area near the top collar and the surface of the iced base board near the base collar can be used to compliment and merge the run-out and cake together by the addition of a series or build-up of linework (3, 2, 1 linework - see page 82) usually following the collar design shape. Fine coloured lines are often used here to highlight the collar. One of the most important considerations to be made when attempting to design run-out collars for cakes is the importance of balance, the width of the run-out in relationship to the size of the cake. It is usually practised that the amount of top border run-out that projects from the cake outwards should be less than the width of the base board, that is the distance between the cake edge and board edge, otherwise if the run-out and board projections are the same, the cake will appear to be 'top heavy' and therefore unbalanced. When commencing to draw a run-out design, first define the size, shape and edge of the cake. For a square cake fig. 117 draw an accurate square shape with sides measuring the same as your cake. If the cake has not yet been marzipanned or iced don't forget to allow for this extra width measurement of the cake base when initially constructing the cake size on paper. Indicate the cake edge or as we shall now refer to it the 'CAKE LINE' by drawing it in with a darker or different coloured line to the rest of the work, or as I do with a dotted line. This will aid drawing so that the designer doesn't become confused with the many other lines which will eventually be on the paper. A round cake design fig. 118 is drawn using a compass to indicate the cake line. One of the next lines to be

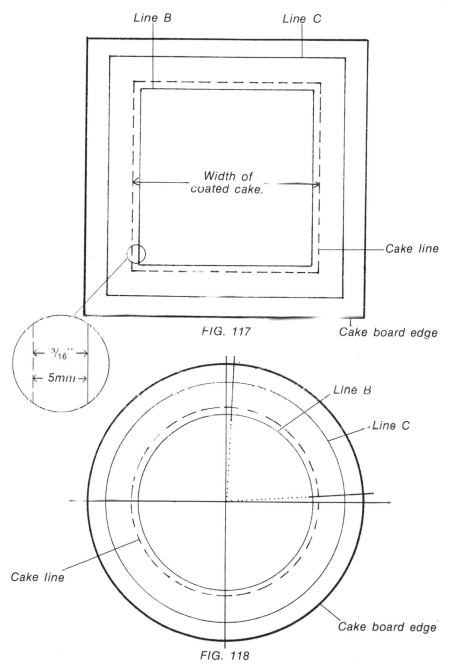

Line B

Line C

Width of
coated cake.

Cake line

FIG. 117

Cake board edge

³/₁₆"

5mm

Line B

Line C

Cake line

Cake board edge

FIG. 118

included on the design is the cake board edge. Normally the size of the cake board to be used is calculated by the addition of 3''/(7½cm) to the overall width of the cake base, giving a border of 1½'' (38mm) around the cake; and 8''/(20cm) cake therefore would require an 11''/(27½cm) base board. The base board of the bottom tier of a wedding cake could be slightly larger. Guidelines for the run-out inside and outside edge can now be drawn in. Lines B and C respectively shown in fig. 117 and 118. Using average cake base sizes for a tiered cake fig. 119 shows the guidelines I would recommend for run-out widths:

6''/(15cm) cake - run out width approx. 1''-1⅛'' 25mm-28mm.

8''/(20cm) cake - run out width approx. 1⅛''-1¼'' 28-31mm.

10''/(25cm) cake - run out width approx. 1¼''-1½'' 31mm-38mm.

These are only approximate width guides and would vary to accommodate each individual design e.g. a run-out with severe curves can be wider than the guidelines in some places, and narrower than the guidelines in other parts - this can be seen in the plan view of a corner run-out fig. 120.

Intermediate sizes of run-out widths can be calculated from the above table. When drawing in the guidelines, indeed with most of the lines, always use faint lines as these most probably will later be erased once an outline for a design has been formed. The portion of run-out to be seated onto the cake top fig. 117 should be no less than ⅛'' (3mm) an average guide is ³⁄₁₆''/(5mm) and no more than ¼''/(6mm) in to the cake from the cake edge line, again, these measurements will also vary with, for instance, a run-out with curved or irregular inside lines. Both the inside and outside guidelines will no doubt sometimes have to be extended or decreased fig. 121 and 122. This is fine, providing a balanced effect can be and is achieved. Also take into account that a 'heavy' or wide run-out with the occasional extremely narrow section will prove to be very fragile and consequently difficult to handle, besides a possibility of an unbalanced effect being created.

It is a good idea to make two drawings of the basic cake shape guidelines plan, one to practice on and experiment with design possibilities, the other to transfer a finalised design onto as a finished plan. Take the practice copy and using a soft pencil rough out some ideas you may have and wish to try using straight and curved lines, or a combination of the two. Here you may well ask yourself, how do I start to design? There are a few ways to start the ideas flowing to produce a design. Obviously, the more experienced you become the easier it will be to create your own original by combining ideas you have noted from displays, books, photographs and exhibitions etc. One way to make a start is to decide upon a certain number of divisions each to have a particular shape within them which is then repeated or alternated to form a complete design. This number of divisions could then be further applied to determine such things as number and spaces of side panels, number of dropped scallop lines on the side of the cake, even the number of spacing of flowers or other motifs to be used to decorate the base board.

FIG. 119
Run-out width guidelines

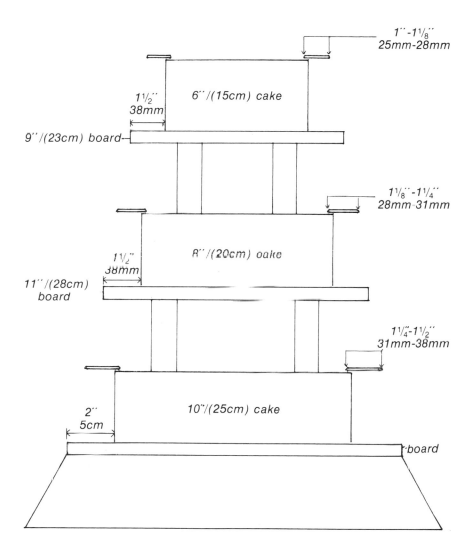

1''-1⅛''
25mm-28mm

1½''
38mm

6''/(15cm) cake

9''/(23cm) board

1⅛''-1¼''
28mm-31mm

1½''
38mm

8''/(20cm) cake

11''/(28cm)
board

1¼''-1½''
31mm-38mm

2''
5cm

10''/(25cm) cake

board

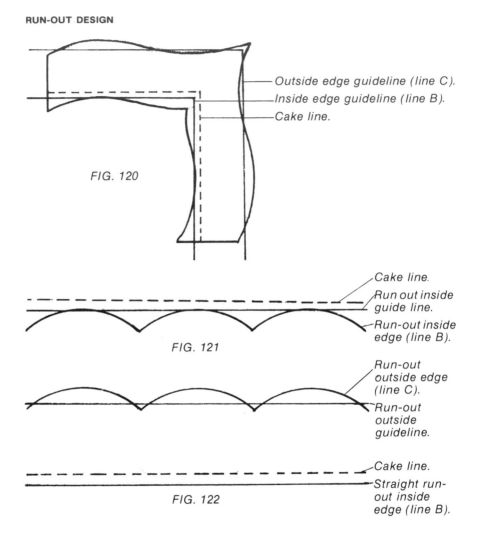

Outside edge guideline (line C).

Inside edge guideline (line B).

Cake line.

FIG. 120

Cake line.

Run out inside guide line.

Run-out inside edge (line B).

FIG. 121

Run-out outside edge (line C).

Run-out outside guideline.

Cake line.

Straight run-out inside edge (line B).

FIG. 122

A cake collar can be sub-divided into a number of divisions or sections ranging from three to thirty, four to thirty two or any other such multiple of a number depending upon the required intricacy of the design. Fig. 123 shows the start of a round cake design divided into four equal sections each section having been sub-divided into with a shape, the same in each, in this case a curve, that when repeated has formed a simple run-out design. This type of design is referred to as a "FULL COLLAR', however, if we now take one of the quarter sections we could execute the shape in royal icing, producing four the same, these would then be re-assembled to form the full design (on the cake) - this type of design method being referred to as 'QUARTER COLLAR'

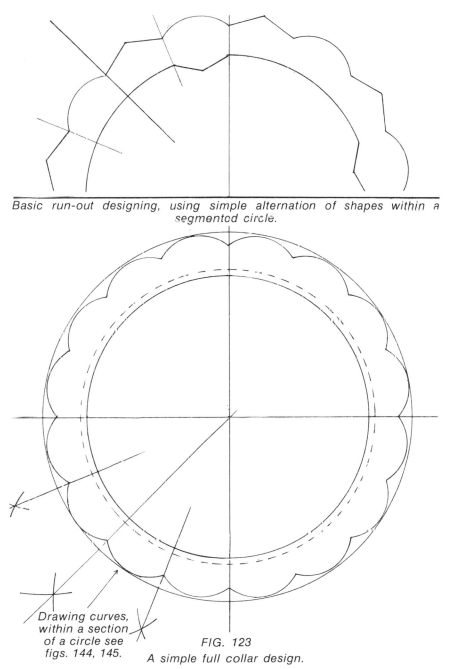

Basic run-out designing, using simple alternation of shapes within a segmented circle.

Drawing curves, within a section of a circle see figs. 144, 145.

FIG. 123
A simple full collar design.

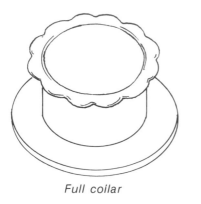

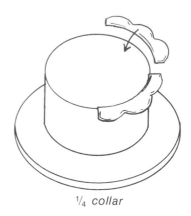

Full collar

$^1/_4$ *collar*

fig. 124, or used on a square cake 'CORNER COLLAR' fig. 125. Another possibility for a square cake is the 'SIDE COLLAR' fig 126 (not corners as previous) with spaces at each corner. The advantages of sectioned collars are discussed later. Another idea to construct your design around is to take a particular shape related to the overall theme of the design or celebration and include this in the run-out shape. This could take the form of for instance a heart for a wedding cake fig. 153 or a bell shape to be included on a Christmas cake run-out. It could also be that you wish to include a floral motif arranged in a semi-circle, a horseshoe or numeral to be mounted on the finished run-out, shapes of any of these features and many more can successfully be used as a basis of your design.

Decide first whether your collar is going to take the form of a full or quarter type design; both look equally attractive in their own individual way when completed. If you choose to use a quarter or corner collar run-out design, small spaces need to be left between each run-out at the point where they would meet, this is to avoid a 'butt' joint and give that little extra amount of tolerance should the cake be fractionally larger or smaller than anticipated after final coating. For competition purposes this could be more accurately gauged, but commercially the space between can be quite helpful when assembling for final decoration fig. 128 shows these spaces, note that on a round cake the end edges of the run-out are designed to radiate from the centre point. In both cases square and round, the spaces are equal on both sides of the quarter dividing line. Spaces of a similar nature are also left on the square cake side type run-out fig. 126. Once the run-out has been designed the edges or ends of each run-out can be made more interesting and indeed better fitting to the design by introducing one of the suggested end shapes from fig. 129. Also shown are ideas for motifs to be included in these spaces to suit various themes, using these the spaces are designed slightly larger to accomodate the features which will become an integrated part of the run-out border. The motifs range from small run-out shapes with over-piping, plastic or hand-made motifs, sugar piped, moulded, plastic or silk flowers to a selection of gold and silver band or velvet ribbon etc. A selection of OVERLAYS are shown, fig. 130 which are an ideal way to fully conceal the spaces. Corner overlays and 'filler motifs' are shown in fig. 131.

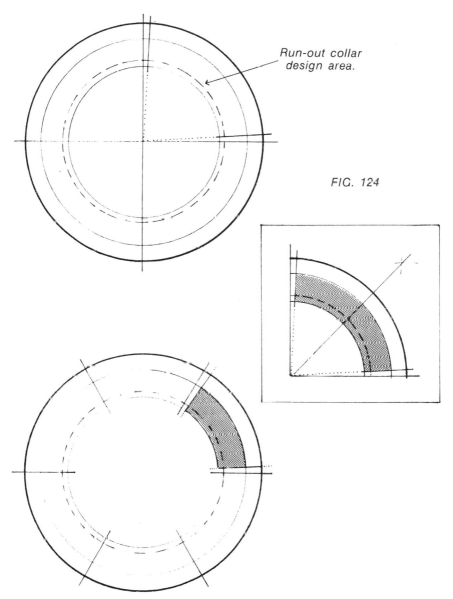

Run-out collar
design area.

FIG. 124

Sectioned collar design area.

Smaller run-outs than ¼ collars can be produced using more divisions as
shown above, especially useful for mult-sided cakes such as hexagon
and octagon shapes see fig. 146.

105

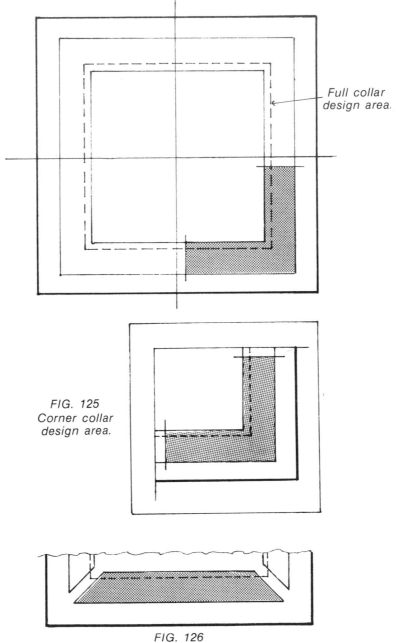

*Full collar
design area.*

*FIG. 125
Corner collar
design area.*

*FIG. 126
Side collar design area.*

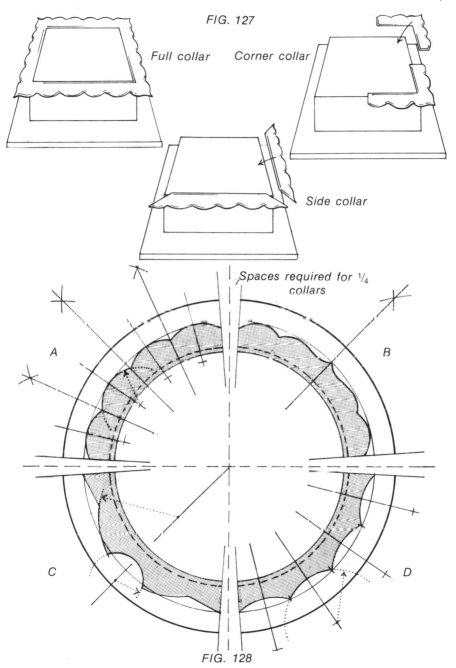

FIG. 127

Full collar   Corner collar

Side collar

Spaces required for ¼ collars

A

B

C

D

FIG. 128

RUN-OUT DESIGN

Run-out end edges.
a

Filler motifs
b

FIG. 129

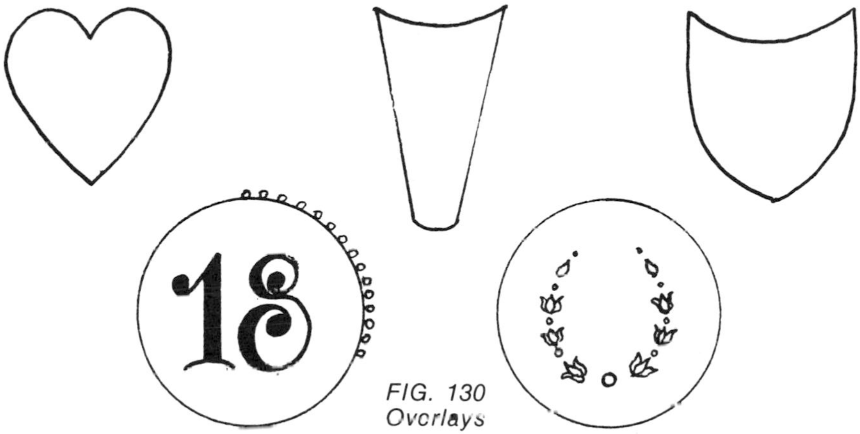

FIG. 130
Overlays

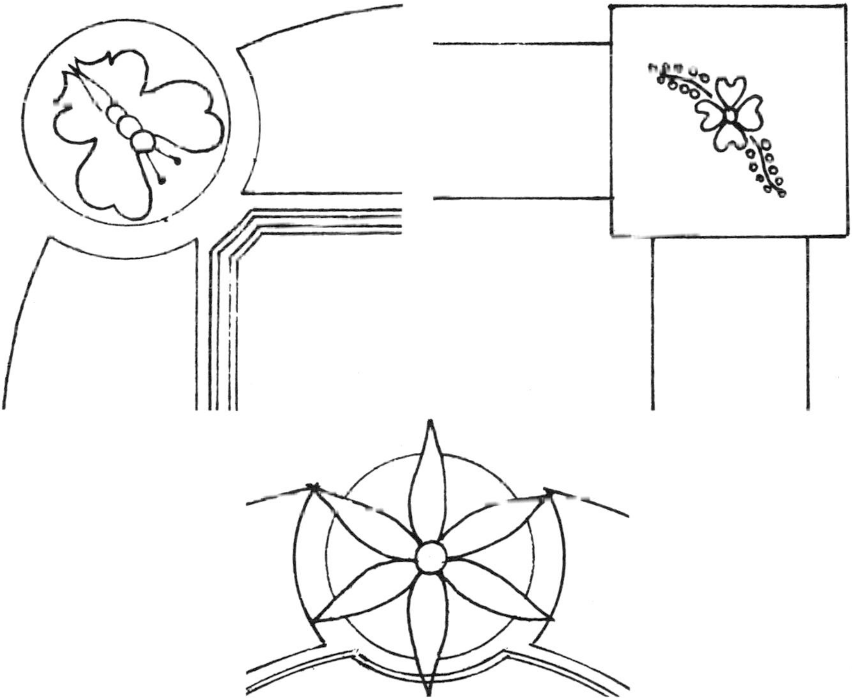

FIG. 131
Corner overlays.

The advantage of quarter run-outs is the reduced risk of possible breakage, the smaller run-out units being easier to handle and assemble onto cakes especially if an intricate, fine design is used. Five quarter run-outs are usually produced in royal icing as a precaution, just in case one should get damaged or soiled. The spare unit would hopefully not be used, however, it is wise to prepare one at the initial stages enabling you to use the same icing colour and consistency to ensure a perfect match should it be needed. To make a spare full collar would obviously require more materials, time and of course extra drying and storage space.

During the design stages, only one quarter run-out design need be drawn in order to be able to outline and reproduce in royal icing, unless of course artwork is required for a fully illustrated cake plan or design assignment, then all four sections would need to be shown. In the case of a full collar, the complete outline is required in all instances. Avoid trying to save time or 'cut corners' by tracing a completed quarter section and fitting four together to form a full design, this can result in several inaccuracies causing problems at the manufacturing stages, it is far neater, more accurate and sometimes quicker in the long run to extensively use drawing instruments when constructing designs, this way one should achieve accuracy in drawing straight and curved lines, the exception to this (in run-out designing) is when a free or irregular curve needs to be repeated on a design. For this we would trace the curve onto tracing paper using a sharp pencil to obtain a clear line, reverse the tracing paper and re-trace the image in the correct position on the design. Ensure accuracy at all times by using markers such as the run-out guidelines with which you started, to re-align the tracing each time. An example of this type of design is shown in fig. 137. Don't draw the curve immediately onto your main design sheet, practice first with a rough sketch on scrap paper until the desired curve is achieved. Irregular curves can also be applied using the template technique described on page 40.

Fig. 128 A and D show simple curve sectioned designs based on the bisection of a circle described on pages 8 and 9. Using the circumference of one of the guideline circles bisect and further bisect and further sub-bisect to produce eight divisions in each quarter of the circle, then using the curve drawing principles on page 127, draw in the required curves. It can be seen that fig. 128 A, B and D, have been constructed within the inside and outside guidelines. Fig. 128 C, however, because of it's wide and narrow variations in width has extended and in certain places been decreased from the basic guideline but still retains an overall balanced appearance.

The inside edge of each of the afore mentioned designs in fig. 128 have been left as a continuous curved line (the inside run-out guidelines). Due to the fact that these are quarter run-outs we can use the space between each to include a break in the linework piping which is added once the run-outs are assembled on the cake, to merge the run-out and cake surface together. Using breaks, in this case not meaning a space but a detail or variation in the linework we can avoid concentric circular piping, which can be difficult to execute accurately without practice and prove very time consuming. Applied correctly, and as an integral part of a good design, concentric piped circular line-work looks quite effective, it is used mainly in exhibition type cake decoration and not normally accepted as being commercially practical. Some examples of details or breaks to include in your design are shown in fig.

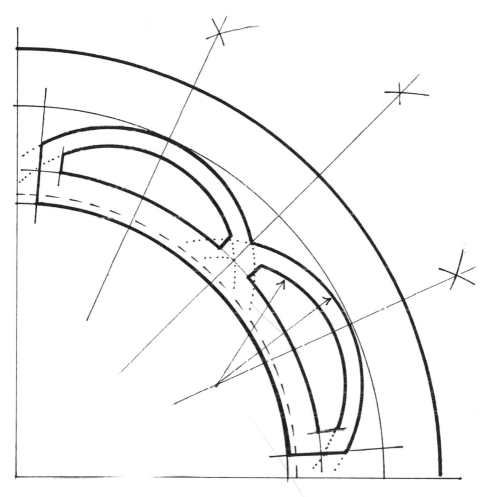

Actual size for 6″/(15cm) cake

FIG. 132
¼ run-out collar design suitable for 6″/(15cm) round cake.
Join four together at the design stage to produce a full collar design.

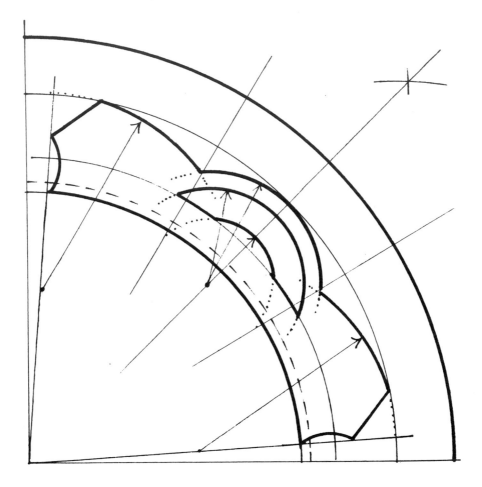

Actual size for 6''/(15cm) cake.

FIG. 133

¼ run-out collar design suitable for 6''/(15cm) round cake.
Join four together at the design stage to produce a full collar design.

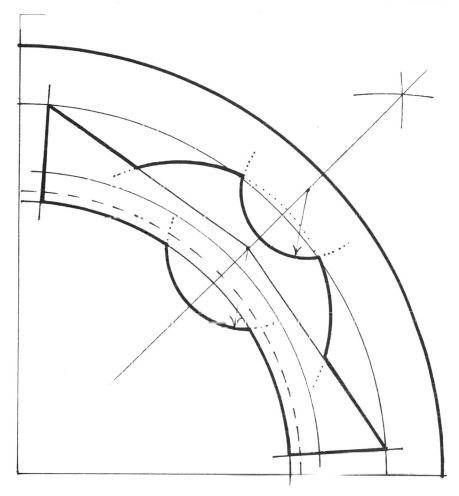

Actual size for 6″/(15cm) cake.

FIG. 134.

¼ run-out collar design suitable for 6″/(15cm) round cake.
Join four together at the design stage to produce a full collar design.

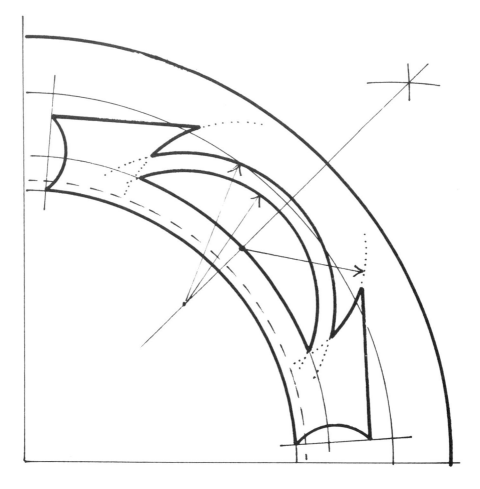

Actual size for 6″/(15cm) cake.

FIG. 135

¼ *run-out collar design suitable for 6″/(15cm) round cake.*
Join four together at the design stage to produce a full collar design.

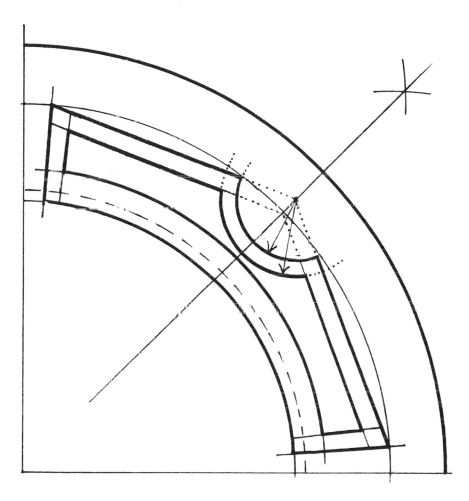

Actual size for 6″/(15cm) cake.

FIG. 136

$1/4$ *run-out collar design suitable for 6″/(15cm) round cake.*
Join four together at the design stage to produce a full collar design.

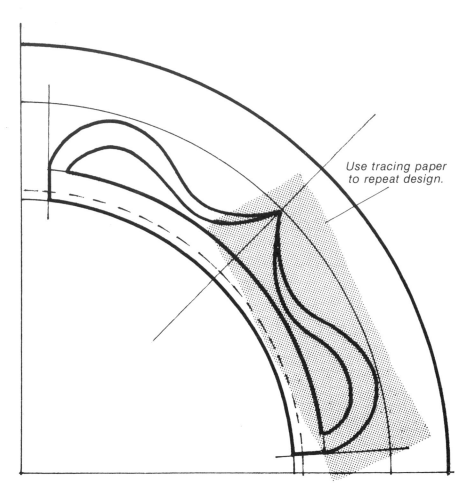

Use tracing paper to repeat design.

Actual size for 6″/(15cm) cake.

FIG. 137

¼ run-out collar design suitable for 6″/(15cm) round cake.
Join four together at the design stage to produce a full collar design.

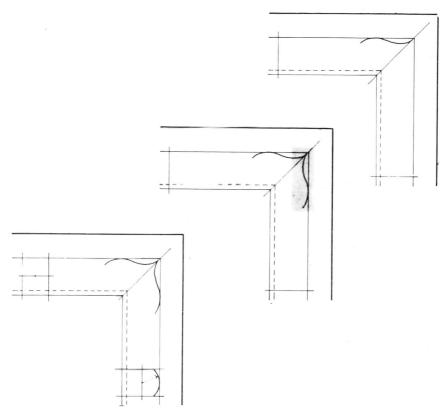

FIG. 138
Corner collar construction for square cakes (completed design is shown below).

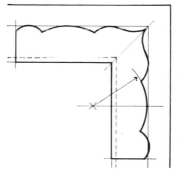

Corner run-out collar design for a square cake. Join four together at the design stage to produce a full collar design.

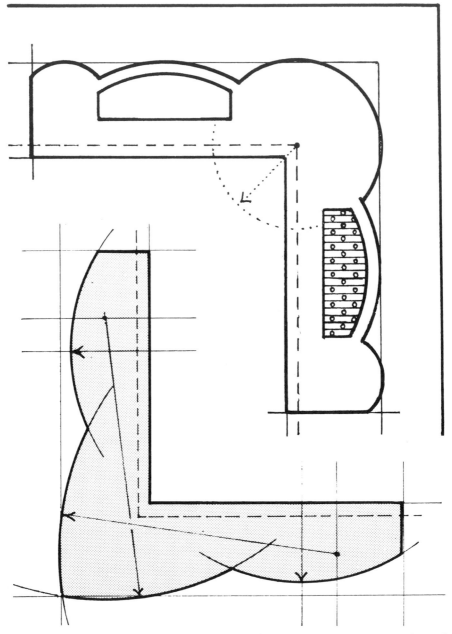

Corner run-out collar designs suitable for 6″/(15cm) square cakes. Join four of the same shape together at the design stage, to produce a full collar design.

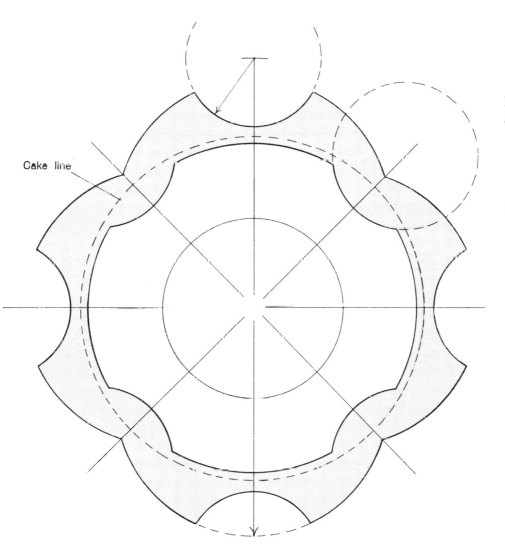

Cake line

Full collar run-out design. Note: Working drawing lines have been retained, to show how the design is constructed.

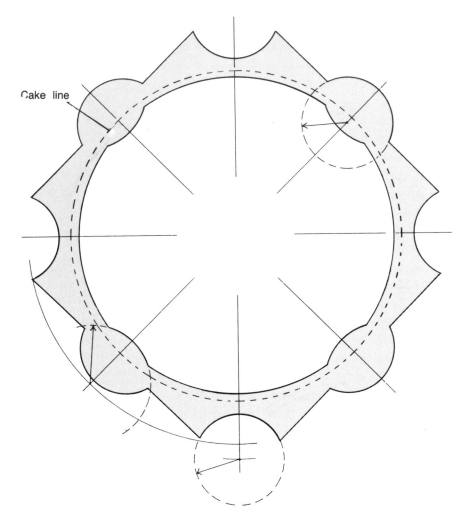

Cake line

Full collar run-out design. Note: Working drawing lines have been retained, to show how the design is constructed.

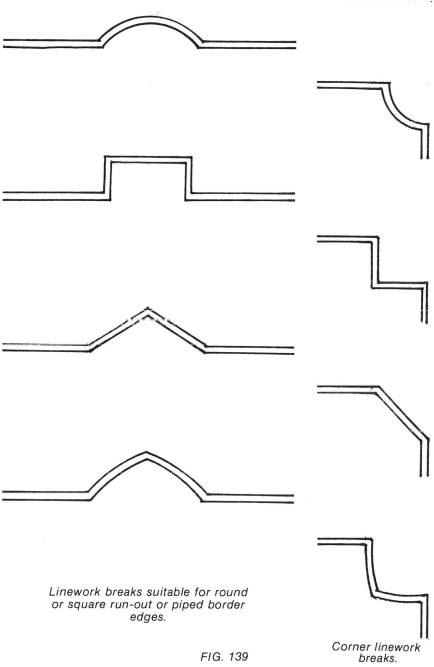

Linework breaks suitable for round
or square run-out or piped border
edges.

FIG. 139

Corner linework
breaks.

RUN-OUT DESIGN

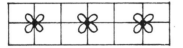

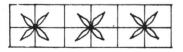

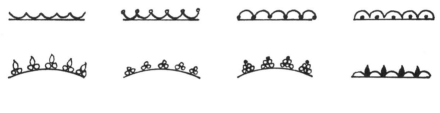

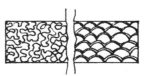

FIG. 140

139. In the case of full collars where no spaces are formed within the run-out, we can include a protruding shape on the inside edge of the run-out at accurately spaced intervals to provide the necessary break in the line work to facilitate easier piping. Figs. 148 to 153 illustrate this.

Most quarter and corner run-outs, even side run-outs can be linked together at the design stage to form a design for a full collar, similarly a full collar could be separated to produce a design for quarter or corner sections. In effect we can create two, may be more different uses from one design. There will no doubt come a time when you will require CUT-OUTS to be included in your run-out designs, these are open sections or spaces within the actual run-out, which compliment and usually follow part of a shape already in the design, making the overall effect of a more delicate and open appearance figs. 132, 133 135, 136 and 137 show collar designs with outlines of cut-out sections. All plain collar designs can be adapted to facilitate cut-outs, therefore one can produce several designs each with different cut-outs and decoration all from one basic outline. The cut-outs may be left empty, enhanced very plainly or emphasised and highlighted by the used of dot formations, line and dot, wrought work, flowers or various other decorative motifs. Some typical shapes and popular cut-out decoration is shown in fig. 140, the dot formations could be used to embellish the inside edge of a cut-out or the outside edge of the run-out collar, used in moderation they can look quite tasteful.

Delicate collars look very nice used with the appropriate colours on a cake to suit the required theme or recipiant, even so remember they should, for commercial purposes be practical. The more elaborate designs should be used for competition work, and the designer must bear this in mind, that there is a vast difference between basic, commercial cake finishing and competition work. In the early stages of your cake designing and decoration, one should, I feel try and design according to ones own practical and design abilities. After all, it will probably be you that is going to reproduce your own designs in edible material, so design, knowing that you will be able to accurately, neatly and proficiently execute the collar design with reasonable ease, at the same time enjoying the work. It is most unwise to design a very fragile, delicate collar if your linework, piping or the filling in or intricate designs with soft icing is found difficult, far better to produce a well finished quality item from a more basic design, until of course one becomes more confident and experienced in designing and execution.

BASE COLLARS

If time and cost allow, and certainly for high class work, base board collars to match the top collar design look most effective and do create a sense of completeness to the overall balance, a total, finished look to the cake. To create this balanced effect when using base board collars it is advisable to increase the width of the collar from the cake edge outwards towards the board edge, (leaving space for linework) therefore making it wider than the top collar (that is the top collar width from the top cake edge outwards). fig. 141 illustrates this. When producing the unit from royal icing one would outline on the design the outer collar edge shape and what we have referred to as the cake line, so this inside edge would be in effect a plain circle or square to fit against the shape of the cake. There are various ways in which this type of base decoration can be introduced onto the cake, each is described to enable you to understand the mechanics of the application in order that you can then select the appropriate methods for a particular use.

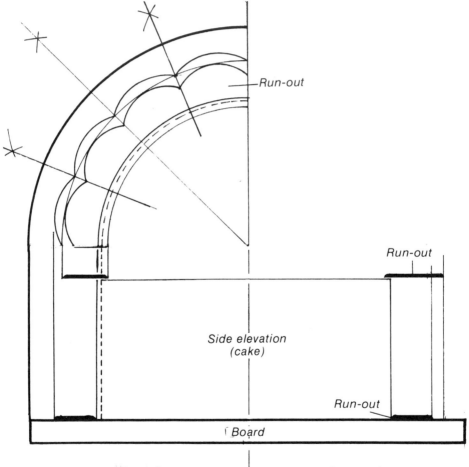

Run-out

Run-out

Side elevation
(cake)

Run-out

Board

Correct.
Balanced appearance.

Incorrect.
'Top heavy' appearance.

FIG. 141

For the first method, fig. 142a and incidentally these are not in any order of preference, prepare the collar as you would for the top; piping and drying on waxed paper. The dried collar would then be attached and centrally aligned on a prepared cake board previously coated with base coloured royal icing, the cake with finished top and side coating would then be positioned inside the run-out and secured with royal icing; this could then be further finished with small pearl type bulb or small shell to neaten the join between the run-out and cake side. This method is only necessary if a full collar is being used, or where the cake is for exhibition work when a perfectly level coated board is normally expected to be shown. If quarter collars are used, fig. 142b, the base board work becomes considerably more simple. Finish the cake top, sides and board in the conventional manner up to and including the final coat of icing then attach the four or more run-out pieces around the base of the cake, again the join of the cake with the run-out would usually be concealed in some way with further decoration. The advantage of this method is if the icing coat is slightly thicker than was anticipated when the design was drawn, in this event the run-outs would still fit the cake but the spaces between would be larger. The filler motifs shown in fig. 129b would then be employed here to complete the border.

Base collars can also be piped and filled directly onto the coated and dried base board, fig. 142c, in which case a template, the same shape as the top collar outer edge, slightly large in size would be required. This could be cut from cartridge paper or thin card (cake box card is ideal). The template is then aligned on the base board, outlined in royal icing and filled in with soft run-sugar, this must then immediately be dried in a rapid

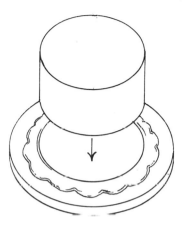

FIG. 142a

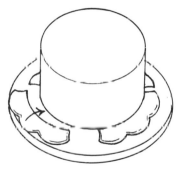

FIG. 142b

FIG. 142c

but gentle heat, the low heat of an anglepoise lamp bulb is ideal and can easily be positioned near the icing. If the drying or at least 'crusting over' process is not fairly rapid there is a potential risk of the soft run-sugar used to fill-in, dissolving the dry base board icing and consequently, slowly causing a collapsed run-out surface with a dull finish, instead of the required smooth, shiny surface. A second risk of moist run-sugar penetrating into, and gradually up the sides of the cake forming an unsightly moisture mark around the cake usually never completely disappearing, even when dry.

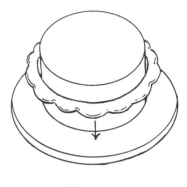

FIG. 142d

Another method to try when producing full collars is to place a prepared dried run-out collar over the top and down the sides of the coated cake and onto the iced cake board fig. 142d. Remember though on square cakes if your coating is not 'squared off' or on round cakes on which has been produced the unacceptable 'lighthouse' or 'funnel' effect the collar will not fit at the base, therefore when using this method ensure that your design specifications and practical work are accurately compatible.

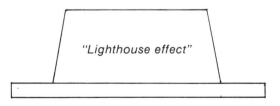

"Lighthouse effect"

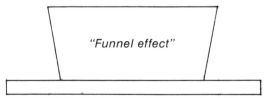

"Funnel effect"

Side elevations showing incorrect coating.

As mentioned previously, when designing and allowing for base collars or run-outs, the width from the cake line (cake side) to the outside edge of the run-out should be larger than that of the top run-out, in order to create added 'weight' to the base of the cake and an overall balance. The extra width required will depend upon the size of cake and of course would be graduated in the case of tiered cakes the measurement could range from an extra $\frac{3}{16}$" for a top tier or 6"/(15cm) approx. up to $\frac{3}{8}$" for a base tier or 10"/(25cm) approx. cake.

To minimise work and eliminate the need for two separate drawings, designs for both top and base run-out can be drawn on one sheet of paper fig. 143. To enable an easier understanding of the procedure for drawing base run-outs the diagram has been divided horizontally into two halves, normally the drawing would be the same in each half. The shaded area in the top half of the drawing shows the area to be outlined and filled in for the top run-out, whilst in the bottom half of the drawing the shaded area represents the area to be outlined and filled-in for the base run-out. The width of the run-out has been increased by simply extending the constructional axis and outlines used for the top run-out outline. Note also the inside edge of the base run-out is the square shape of the cake just fractionally larger than the cake line, to allow for any slight inaccuracies in the icing.

An optional variation is that the cut-outs used in the top run-out have been omitted on the base run-out to allow for the inclusion of decorations such as flowers, horseshoes etc., on the surface. Linework would be piped on the base board parallel to the outside run-out edge, allow for this when extending the collar size bearing in mind the conventional board size calculation on page 100.

Curves within sections of a circle or square are frequently used as a basis of a run-out outline shape. The acuteness of the curve within the section can be varied quite simply by extending or reducing the radius, therefore providing scope for several variations from one basic outline. The technique is illustrated in fig. 144. Keeping the pencil point on the circumference B and the point of the compass at A a slight curve is featured within the section (note the centre point line in each section has been obtained using bisection page 8). If we now move clockwise around the circle with the pencil point being kept on the circumference and the radius, centred in each segment continually reduced then each curve becomes more severe until reaching the small full circle.

Fig. 144b shows the same exercise for use on square edges.

Fig. 145a illustrates the formation of a cut-out segment based on a circular section, keep the compass point in the same place and reduce the radius accordingly.

Fig. 145b a curve opposite within a curve.

Fig. 145c a less curve shape, keep the pencil in the same place on the centre line and increase the radius.

Fig. 145d techniques a, b, and c combined.

127

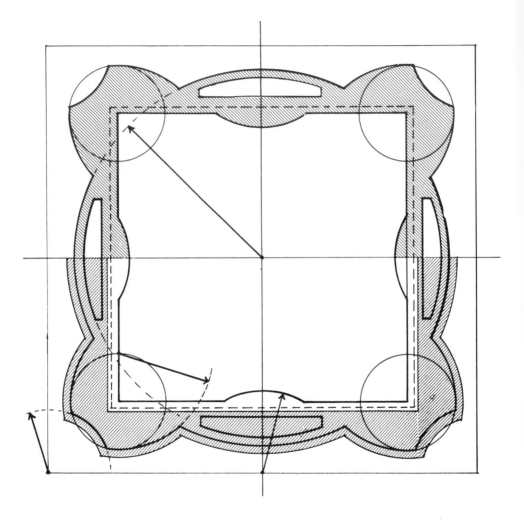

FIG. 143

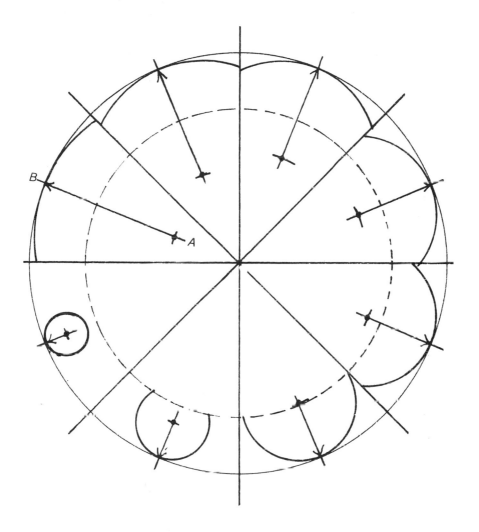

FIG. 144

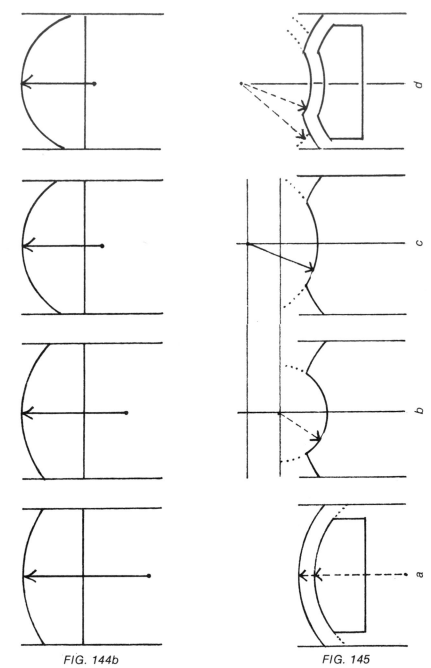

FIG. 144b

FIG. 145

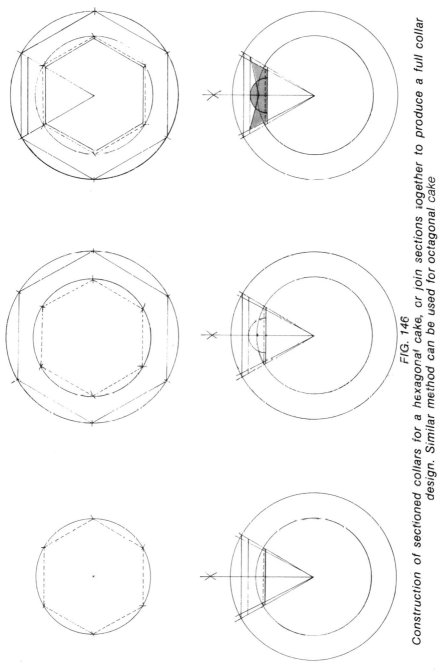

FIG. 146
Construction of sectioned collars for a hexagonal cake, or join sections together to produce a full collar design. Similar method can be used for octagonal cake

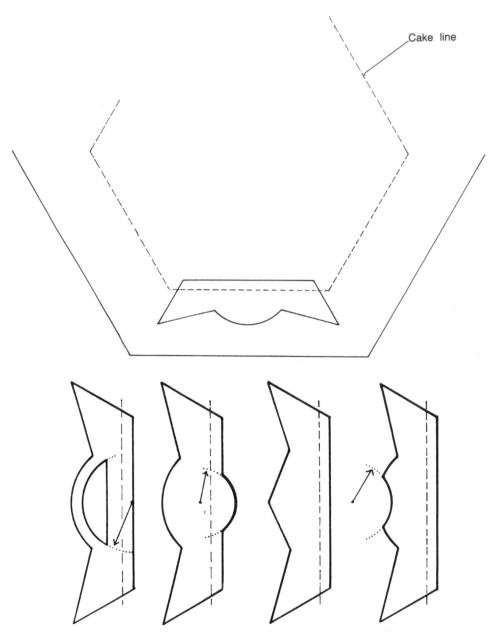

Cake line

FIG. 146
Variations on basic design for sectioned collars - hexagonal cake.

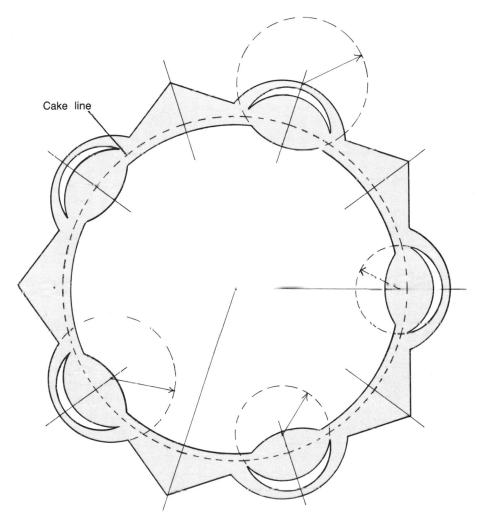

Cake line

Full collar run-out design. Note: Working drawing lines have been retained, to show how the design is constructed.

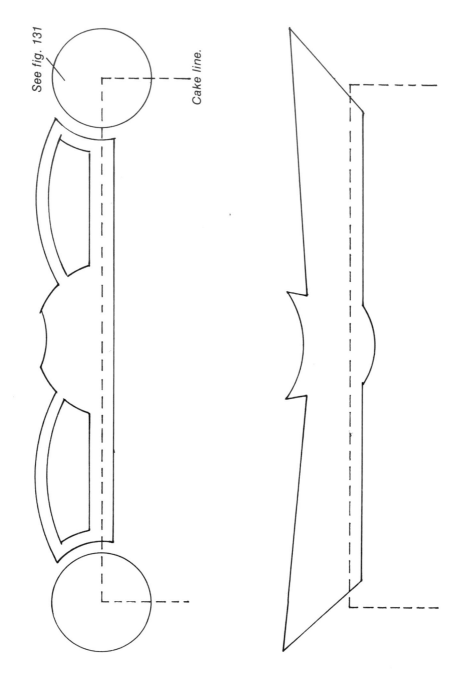

See fig. 131

Cake line.

134

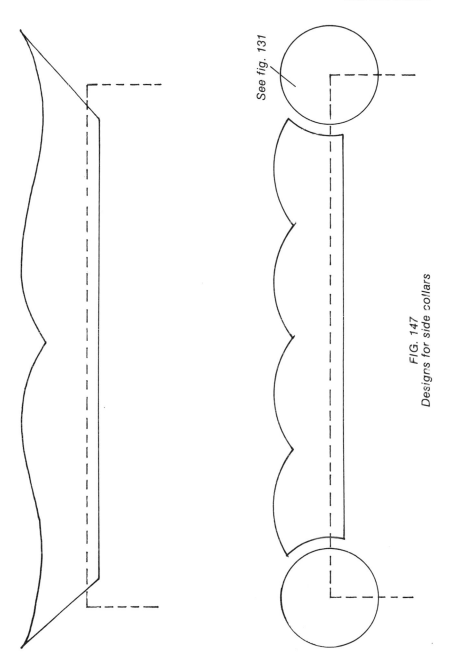

See fig. 131

FIG. 147
Designs for side collars

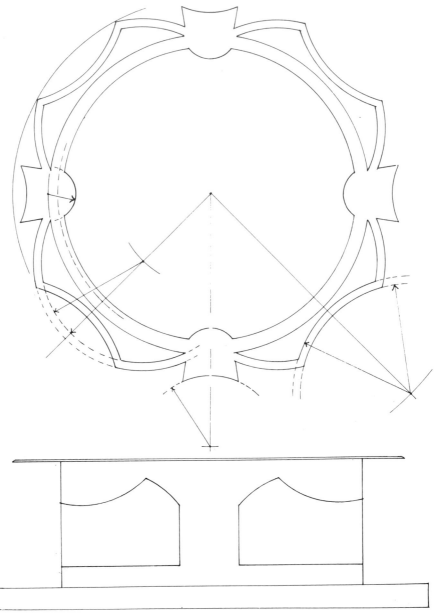

FIG. 148
*Full collar run-out design. Note: Working drawing lines have been retained, to
show how the design is constructed.
Side panel linework design to match top collar outline.*

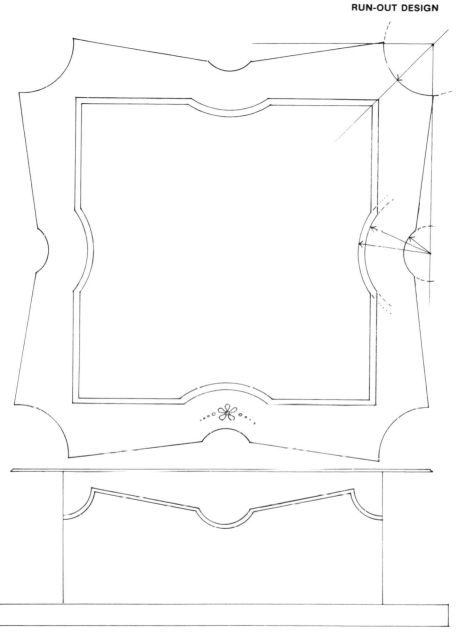

FIG. 149

*Full collar run-out design. Note: Working drawing lines have been retained, to
show how the design is constructed.
Side panel linework design to match top collar outline.*

137

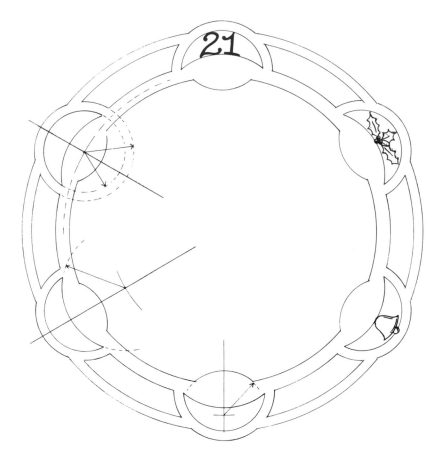

FIG. 150

Full collar run-out design. Note: Working drawing lines have been retained, to show how the design is constructed.

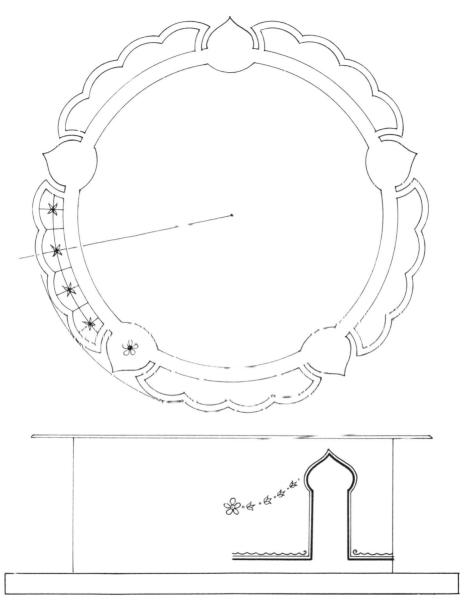

FIG. 151

Full collar run-out design. Note how piped lines in cut-out sections are drawn to radiate from the centre point.
Side linework design to incorporate shape used in collar design.

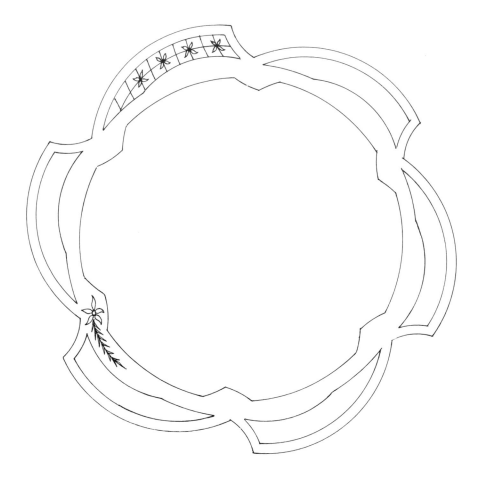

FIG. 152

Full collar run-out design. Note: Working drawing lines have been retained, to show how the design is constructed.

FIG. 153

Full collar run-out design. Note: Working drawing lines have been retained, to show how the design is constructed.

FIG. 154

*Full collar run-out design. Floral motifs have been included in order to illustrate
a few design ideas.*

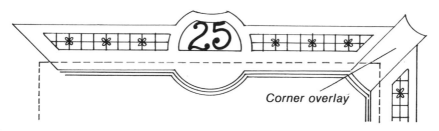

Corner overlay

Full side collar with cut-out sections, suitable for square or rectangular shaped cake.

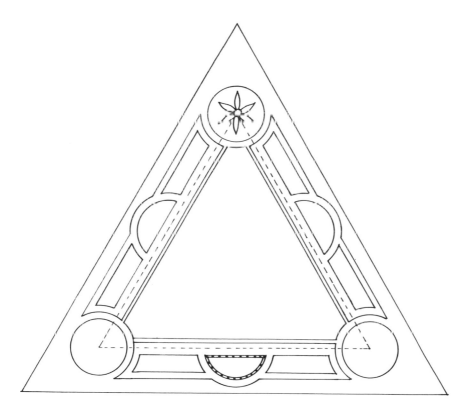

Full side collar design for triangular shaped cake.

FIG. 155

FIG. 156
Double run-out collar with cut-out sections.

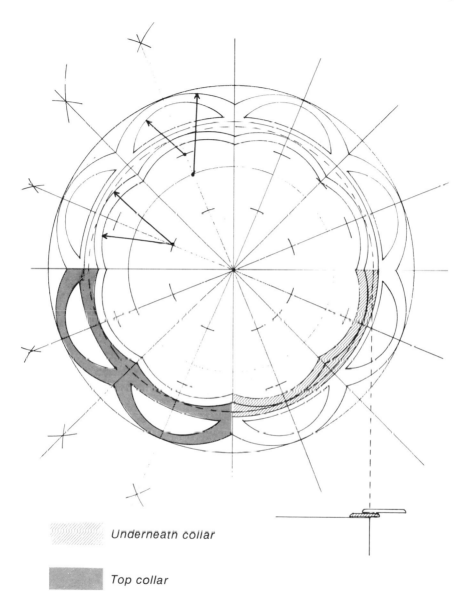

Underneath collar

Top collar

FIG. 156a
Construction of design for double run-out collar.

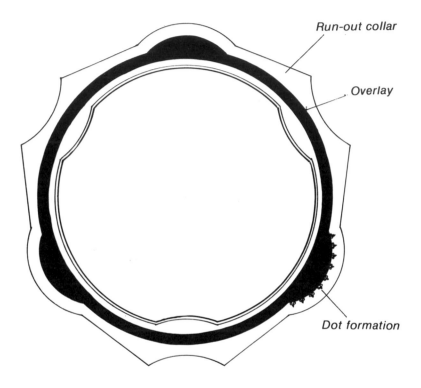

FIG. 157
Full run-out collar with overlay.

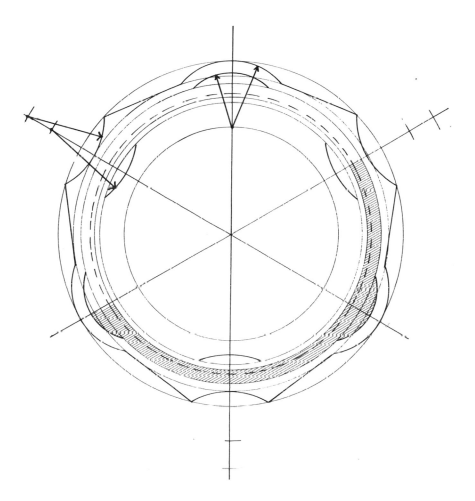

FIG. 157a
Construction of design for full run-out collar with overlay.

147

DOUBLE COLLARS

Once run-out design and manufacture has been practiced sufficiently, the designer may be looking for a more adventurous or unusual method of utilizing basic run-out principles. An interesting variation is the DOUBLE COLLAR, the double collar as the name suggests consists of two prefabricated run-out pieces used in conjunction with each other. They can add tremendous variety, and assist the designer in producing something out of the ordinary to include in his range of designs. Fig. 156 illustrates a double collar, the shaded area representing a second collar beneath the top collar shown as the plain area. Fig. 156a shows the design stages required to achieve the effect. The lighter shaded area is the collar attached to the cake top (see side elevation view) the outside edge is protruding fractionally over the cake line (cake edge) far enough to aid the support of the top collar, however, not as far as to be seen through the cut-out sections included within the design. The inside edge is further in to the centre of the cake top than the edge of the top collar, and is the same shape and parallel to the top run-out edge.

The darker shaded are is the top collar (shown plain in fig. 156).

The top run-out inside edge and the second or base run-out need not be parallel, and the same shape as in fig. 149 and fig. 154, in fact some attractive designs can be developed by tapering or graduating the inside edge, even using a quite 'contrasty' shape against the top run-out, providing a balanced appearance is achieved almost anything goes!

The two collars are manufactured separately in the same colour or, to add even more interest, in a contrasting or harmonious colours, they could also be produced by outlining in a different colour to that of the icing used for filling in the run-out.

OVERLAYS

Fig. 157 shows yet another variation of the run-out collar, this being the OVERLAY. Again two separate run-out pieces are assembled together, enabling the design and production of an interesting and skilful piece of decoration. Overlays can be made in the same colour of icing as the underneath run-out, however a different colour does make the unit stand out more. The width of the overlay is considerably less than that of the underneath run-out and should not be made to appear too heavy, both run-out and overlay shape should compliment each other.

Variations from one basic design can be made using alternative colour schemes, thus producing several ideas from one basic outline. The colours used would obviously be determined as usual by the occasion for which the cake is intended.

For both OVERLAY or base collar of a DOUBLE COLLAR try:
Spraying with GOLD colour;
Spraying with SILVER colour;
Spraying with colour, using the aerograph.

For OVERLAY only or single conventional collar:
Red, chocolate or even green overlay, on a white run-out (or suitable pastel tint) with a white 'snow' effect, peaked delicately on and evenly around the overlay. The snow effect could also be lightly dredged with caster sugar to give added sparkle. Marbling effects using coloured icings within the overlay to produce leaves, flowers and various continuous line patterns etc.

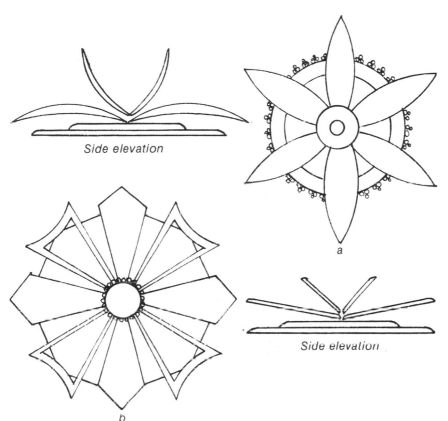

Side elevation

a

Side elevation

b

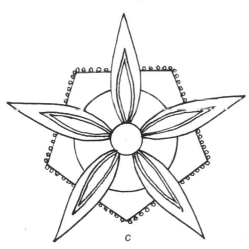

c

FIG. 158
Designs (plans and side elevations)
for cake centrepiece/ornaments,
drawn using basic geometric
principles, tracing and template
techniques described in previous
chapters, to be excecuted in the form
of:-

a. Stencilled royal icing petals on
   double, graduated run-out discs
   with dot edging.

b. Run-out petal and run-out base,
   bulb and dot centre.

c. Run-out base with dot edging,
   stencilled full petals and piped
   open petals on top.

Petal curves and positions can be
varied.

Remembering the point made earlier in the book, regarding the fact that one should design in accordance to ones own practical ability, if your line piping or the line piping of the person manufacturing your designs isn't particularly accurate, then avoid dark coloured outlines for double collars, overlays or conventional run-outs for that matter unless absolutely necessary, otherwise there is a tendancy for the lightness of the icing used to fill-in the run-out to emphasize any inaccuracies in the darker outline, such as curves with 'kinks' in or clumsy joints. It would be far better to outline and fill-in with the same or similar coloured icing, at least until piping proficiency has improved, thus avoiding any of the afore mentioned risks.

Accurate drawing and piping is essential for good run-out work, a good drawing using clean, fine lines makes for a more accurate outline at the manufacturing stages. Variations in width of lines on for instance a double collar design that is intended to be parallel will affect the finished appearance considerably, especially if two contrasting colours are used, which would inevitably emphasize any irregularities.

CHAPTER 10

Lettering

After spending valuable time, and taking considerable care to neatly coat a cake, apply a piped or run-out border and a suitable motif, figure or floral arrangement, cakes are often spoiled when it comes to applying lettering or inscriptions. More often than not this part of cake decoration is the downfall of many confectioners, either because of insufficient knowledge or indeed practice, the unsuitable choice of style, size and colour and the use of incorrect spacing very often spoils what should have been an attractive clean looking cake. This unbalanced, untidy use of inscriptions can be seen in many bakers shop windows displaying celebration cakes reflecting an obvious lack of thought and preparation on the part of the cake decorator.

Previous to applying inscriptions or numerals to a design and then onto a finished product, take time always to consider the elementary principles that follow all of which should be borne in mind when using lettering.

Many of the letters we are familiar with today originate from the Roman alphabet. The confectioner designer should therefore become acquainted with the proportions of these letters before attempting to use more ornate styles or even design ones own style.

It can be seen from fig. 160 that the letters of the Roman alphabet can be divided into four groups:

1. Width three quarters of height.
2. Width half or less of height.
3. Width equal to height.
4. Width more than height.

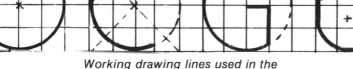

Working drawing lines used in the construction of Roman lettering.

VARIATIONS

Using the basic Roman alphabet we can now progress on to the addition of various ornamentation to make the lettering more interesting.

The first example fig. 160a is an increased thickness of one stroke on each letter, it is important that all thickened strokes are consistent to each letter, usually the left hand vertical stroke and the angled stroke falling away to the right of the letter.

Width equal
to height

Width ¾
of height

Width ½
of height

Width more
than height.

FIG. 159
Roman alphabet.

a
Increased thickness of one stroke.

b
All strokes thickened.

c
All strokes thickened with two different widths.

d
Embellishment.

e
Serifs.

FIG. 160
Variations of Roman alphabet.

By thickening all strokes fig. 160b we obtain quite a bold type of letter ideally suited to run-out work described later. We can also thicken all strokes using two different thicknesses, based on the earlier described principle, to maintain a consistency of thin and thick strokes throughout each letter fig. 160c. All this ornamentation lends itself to further embellishment fig. 160d illumination which will be explained later.

Serifs are frequently used in lettering to add further interest. The serif is a form of decoration on lettering appearing at the end of main strokes of the letter. Examples of serifs are shown in fig. 160e. Remember when introducing serifs into your lettering designs ensure that they can be reproduced in the decorative medium to be used.

SPACING

After mastering the proportions of letters the confectioner designer should then make himself aware of the need to correctly space letters within a word, and words within a phrase.

Spacing is probably the most important aspect of lettering, even the best drawn and balanced letters forming a word can look entirely disjointed if spacing is not correct. The rule is not to space the letters equally but to space them to appear with equal intervals between each letter. Fig. 161a shows a word with equal spacing between letters. Fig. 161b shows the same word with spacing correctly used to give the effect of an equal interval of space between each letter, thus creating a pleasing continuity to the word.

Because of the shape of letters L,A,T,V,C, they have more space around them than most other letters of the alphabet, so when using these very little extra space between them is required. In the case of the letters L and A as in the examples in fig. 162 and fig. 163, these letters can almost touch with no spacing required due to the area of space already created around both letters.

Three of these spacious letters appear in fig. 162a at the end of the word chocoLATe where it can be seen that by reducing the area of space between them an acceptable effect of spacing is achieved fig. 162b, note also the O C O in fig. 162a which can also be brought closer together as in the correct example fig. 162b.

Another example of spacing is shown in fig. 163a with the letters A and V which create a large area of space around themselves when spaced equally, but appear correctly spaced in fig. 163b when positioned closer together.

FIG. 161a

FIG. 161b

FIG. 162a

FIG. 162b

FIG. 163a

FIG. 163b

SIZE

The size of the cake will obviously determine the size of lettering that one can employ, the smaller cake being more suited to small directly piped or semi-illuminated type inscription using fine piping tubes, whereas large cakes will carry the more bold run-out or cut marzipan or sugar paste letters.

At the design stages always consider lettering along with the other decoration to be included on the cake top, to enable you to allow yourself sufficient space and the correct shape of area required around say a motif or floral arrangement in which to fit your chosen type of lettering. Keep the message simple, to the point, yet meaningful. Try to avoid over long phrases and groups of words unless the customer particularly wants this or if you are finishing a novelty cake, decorative scroll or piped verse etc., which anyway would have to be piped relatively small.

Plan lettering 'off the cake' until you gain enough confidence to picture the finished design in your mind and produce the same in practice. For competition work however I strongly recommend planning every part of the design off the cake, to reduce the risk of making mistakes on the finished product, commercially a design for every single cake ordered would obviously be impractical, so in industry a confectioner would be expected to pipe more or less directly on to cakes using his or her experience to plan the overall effect in their mind and transfer this in to practice to produce a saleable product.

155

Lack of experience or indeed thought and preparation can sometimes result in letters towards the end of a word being compressed because of insufficient space being allocated on the cake.

This narrowing of letters can with experience be practised and used as a technique to develop your own style and indeed ease the situation in the event of space shortage, the letters are elongated, narrowed, or even bits chopped off some strokes to facilitate fitting a letter into a word, or a word into a space, fig. 164.

FIG. 164

COLOUR

Colour choice of lettering will play a very important part in the design and total finished look of the product, if can often spoil the item rather than improve or compliment the overall appearance if not used with care.

Several options can be considered when choosing colours:

The lettering can be executed in all the same colour.

The main, or most important part of the inscription such as the name or age of the person could be made to stand out from the rest by using a stronger colour for this part than the rest of the inscription or greeting.

The colour of the lettering could be one that has already been used in the design elsewhere such as the coloured line often used to overpipe linework.

Use a colour completely different to any used on the cake to make it really stand out from everything else.

Lettering in the same colour as the base colour of decoration can look quite effective, for instance a white cake with lettering piped on in white, say for a silver wedding anniversary. This type of lettering is subtly attractive being seen clearly only by the shadows cast from it on to the cake surface.

In all instances, when using lettering be most careful not to distract too much from the decoration, centrepiece or painted plaque etc., in order that an overall sense of balance and completeness is achieved.

STYLE

It is always wise to select a style of lettering which is suited for the particular occasion or recipiant of the cake, a commonly referred to example of this is the accepted association of "Old English" type lettering with Christmas cakes. Widely used by the greeting card industry on cards for the festive season. Style of lettering should also suit the recipiant of the cake, a good example of this is a child's or elderly persons cake where the lettering should be legible and easily recognizable. In the case of a child's cake, here the confectioner can use simple bold uncluttered block lettering and also experiment with brighter colours which children are attracted to, rather than the more subtle colours one would normally use on most other cakes.

METHODS OF APPLICATION

1. Directly piped.
2. Run-out.
3. Cut marzipan or sugarpaste.
4. Illuminated.
5. Stencilled.
6. Pre-fabricated plaques.

Combination of two or more of the above.

DIRECTLY PIPED

Directly piped lettering can be the most difficult type of lettering to apply to a cake surface for most people, as once the lettering has been piped onto the cake surface, in the event of a mistake it can in some cases be difficult to remove and correct successfully, especially when darker colours are being used on light backgrounds or base colours. To overcome this problem, the following methods are all worth experimenting with, to enable you to decide upon the easiest way to apply lettering until you become more proficient.

Copy the lettering or figures onto greaseproof paper in pencil, but instead of using a pencil to transfer the mark onto the cake surface, use a fine needle, pin or compass point and outline carefully. In this way only a fine, faint line will be made being easy to cover. Avoid however, scratching the surface too much otherwise this could allow certain mediums and colour preparations to penetrate beneath the surface and 'run' resulting in a blurred effect. After tracing, pipe over the outlines as described

A commonly practised method, which incidentally can be used in conjunction with the above tracing technique until more confidence is gained and a tracing is not required, is to pipe the lettering first in base coloured icing to match the surface onto which the lettering is to be applied, then if a mistake is encountered it can immediately be removed by lifting off with a fine clean paintbrush without leaving a mark, imagine for yourself the result had a mistake occured using bright red or chocolate on a white cake. Once you have achieved a balanced and correctly spaced inscription it can then be overpiped following the base colour line with a finer tube containing the required colour of icing. Using this method there is little risk of soiling the cake surface.

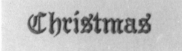

Old English

Directly piped lettering with top half overpiped

Script

Script

Examples of directly piped lettering.

Using a template is an excellent way of providing guidelines within which to pipe to aid the positioning and application of lettering, especially directly piped lettering. Incidentally this technique may be successfully used in conjunction with, or after the decoration arrangement method described on page 57. Prepare a piece of cartridge or tracing paper (cartridge is preferable, tracing may curl during use) the same size and shape as the cake top. Write the required inscription, name and or numeral in the correct place, then outline reasonable closely around the shape of the lettering, cut-out the shape to leave the outline. Align the template onto the cake top and proceed to pipe the required lettering within the guideline shape.

Lettering templates.

RUN-OUT

Examples are shown on page 162 of letters suitable to run-out. Note the use of a bolder type of letter being able to be produced with a smooth surface. Bold type lettering can be produced using the previous direct piping method to form a build-up of lines fig. 165. Equally this run-out method of lettering can be used to create some quite tasteful fine or graduated type lettering. (See page 191 and 193).

Once a design has been decided upon, place conveniently sized pieces of waxed paper over the drawing of the letters, outline with royal icing and then fill in with a softer consistency of icing (let down with a little albumen or water) allow the letters to dry as for conventional run-out work, then peel off the waxed paper and arrange on the cake attaching them with dots of icing. Variations on this type of lettering fig. 166 include:

Outlining in one colour and filling in with a different colour.

Outlining and filling in using the same colour, leave like this or, when dry spray the top or the bottom half with colour using an aerograph spray gun to achieve a faded tone effect.

Use gold or silver spray to finish the dried lettering.

The advantage of this type of prefabricated lettering is that no marks are made on the cake, all the work is prepared 'off cake' and when certain it is correct, placed on the cake.

FIG. 165
Directly piped lettering.

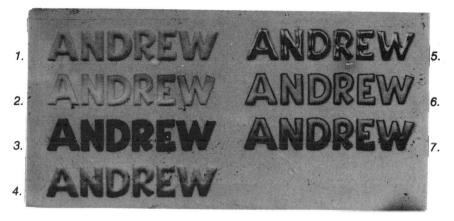

FIG. 166

VARIATIONS OF RUN-OUT LETTERING FROM ONE BASIC STYLE

1. Outline and fill-in with same colour.
2. Spray with colour from top.
3. Dark coloured outline and fill-in.
4. Spray with colour from base.
5. Gold or silver.
6. Dark coloured outline, lighter coloured fill-in icing.
7. As for 6 with colour sprayed from base.

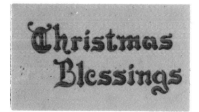

Outline coloured gold before filling in with run-out icing.

Examples of run-out lettering.

Block lettering suitable for run-out work.

Run-sugar lettering can with icing of the correct consistency also be successful piped without an outline, shown in fig. 167. Variations can be made by tapering off the ends of letters or by adding serif type embellishments with the aid of a fine paintbrush.

Spray techniques will further enhance the finished lettering, using halfway sprayed colours or gold, silver etc., to extend the variety.

FIG. 167
Run-out lettering without an outline, piped onto waxed paper or directly onto the cake surface.

CUT MARZIPAN OR SUGARPASTE

Colour the medium being used i.e. marzipan or sugarpaste, then roll out with a rolling pin to the thickness or approximately $\frac{1}{8}$th'' to $\frac{1}{16}$th'' depending on the style and size of the lettering and the cake size. Then 'polish' the surface with the palm of your hand (free from dusting material such as icing sugar) to 'clean' and brighten the appearance of the paste rather than using it with patches of white icing sugar on. I have seen so many cakes with marzipan or sugarpaste left with dusting material on making them look old, stale and generally unattractive in appearance that I always instill into my students this little extra finishing touch so often negelected but making such a difference to a product.

Using a clean knife or ruler and a selection of round and oval cutters one can cut out squares, oblongs, triangles, quarter and semi circles to produce a full alphabet and numerals fig. 169 which in turn can be used to compile inscriptions and names etc. The lettering can be made more appealing by rolling with a ribbed or boxwood rolling pin before cutting out the shapes, this provides interesting textures and patterns on the surface. Remember though to use the lines either all vertically, horizontally or at the same angle when finally positioning the lettering on the cake. Metal letter and number cutters are available for this type of work to simplify the process and make it more commercial.

FIG. 168

FIG. 169
Lettering suitable for cut marzipan or sugarpaste.

Examples of texture and spraying on cut marzipan lettering.

Allow the paste shapes to 'crust over' to ease handling and avoid distortion, then arrange on the cake surface ensuring of course to align, balance and space them correctly before securing with dots of icing.

ILLUMINATED LETTERING

This can provide interest to what would have been a relatively plain style of lettering. Based on the ancient manuscript lettering illumination in this form is to further decorate or embellish, it is usual to illuminate the first letter of a word, (as in a manuscript paragraph), however, providing the embellishment is not too "fussy" it is possible to create attractive inscriptions by illuminating each individual letter, and in some cases this is often the only decoration required on say a fruit layer or bar cake.

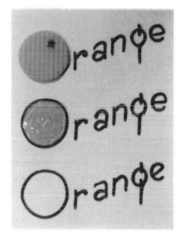

ILLUMINATED OR EMBELLISHED LETTERING

Top: Rib rolled orange marzipan circle.
Centre: Outline filled in with orange piping jelly.
Bottom: Conventional directly piped lettering.

A selection of inscriptions featuring illuminated letters is shown on page 166. Illuminated letters can be produced from several decorative mediums:

Plain chocolate outline, filled in with milk chocolate or vice versa.

Fine chocolate or other coloured fondant lines filled in with coloured piping jellies or coloured fondant.

Royal icing run-out sprayed with an aerograph gun and food colouring, then embellished with fine lines, dots, or miniature floral motifs piped on.

Use of royal icing dot combinations, wavy or scalloped scratched lines along side direct piped lettering.

STENCILLED

Stencils can be used as an aid to the quick and accurate production of inscriptions, being applied directly to the cake surface by means of royal icing or colour applied via and aerograph spray gun. This subject area is covered fully in Chapter 12 Stencilling.

PREFABRICATED PLAQUES

Various inscriptions may be stencilled onto almond paste or sugarpaste plaques of different shapes, sizes and colours using royal icing or the aerograph spray brush method.

Another lettering form can be produced from prepared sugarpaste squares, oblongs or even circles, allowed to dry and then piped up with coloured royal icing or piping chocolate with letters of the alphabet. These can then be stored ready for use and assembled onto the cake to form the required inscription. If keeping a stock of these for commercial use it is advisable to keep the lettering colour the same on a selection of background colours fig. 170.

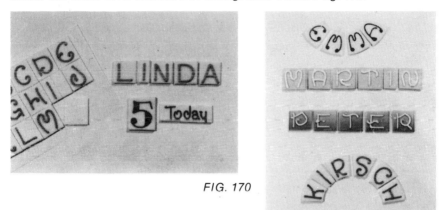

FIG. 170

Lettering plaques with stencilled (sprayed) and directly piped lettering.

Sugarpaste letters using alphabet cutters.

*Lettering plaques with sprayed and icing stencilled lettering, **also** directly piped lettering.*

MONOGRAMS

Defined as two or more letters usually a persons initials combined in one design. Monograms give a more personalised finish to a cake especially popular on Bride cakes when the initials of the Bride and Bride-Groom are entwined and used to decorate the sides of one or more tiers. Monograms can also be used on wedding anniversary and engagement cakes etc.

Several lettering styles lend themselves to monogram work in particular, the Lombardic style fig. 172 which can be executed in run-out and the script type lettering page 192, being suited to the direct piping method of application.

A useful method to employ when designing combined lettering to form a monogram is to trace each of the required letters onto separate pieces of greaseproof or tracing paper, then overlap these and move them around, being semi-transparent you can then experiment with different permutations of the grouping until the most pleasing effect is obtained. Allow the letters to cross over in a least one place and create a comfortable appearance so as not to give the impression that the letters are only just hanging on to each other. Keep all letters in a particular monogram in one direction either vertical or at an angle.

168

 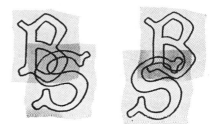

Make tracings of the required letters.

Re-arrange the tracings to achieve the most pleasing balanced effect.

Trace required arrangement ready for use.

DESIGNING A MONOGRAM

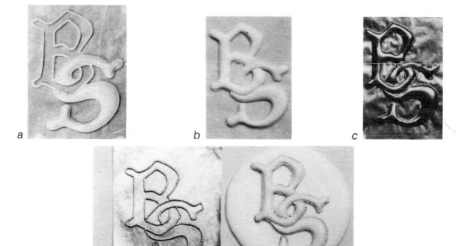

a

b

c

d

PIPING A MONOGRAM

a. Outline letters using one colour, or a different colour for each letter.

b. Fill-in with run-out icing again in one colour or two different colours. Allow the first letter to dry before filling in the other.

c. Finishing variations could include the use of gold or silver colour once the icing is dry.

d. Before filling in with colours such as blue and pink for the letters, colour the piped outline gold or silver to give a very attractive edging.

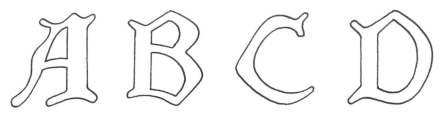

FIG. 171

Medium size
Lombardic style lettering.

Monogram mounted on a plaque
with dot edging.

Dark outline with lighter
fill-in icing.

172

FIG. 172

*Large size
Lombardic style lettering.*

FIG. 173

Small size Lombardic style lettering
used to produce monograms.

174

The prepared design would then be executed as for run-out lettering, filling in the sections which should appear farthest away from you, allow them to 'crust' over then complete the filling in with the parts nearest to you. Experiment with various embellishments spraying and combinations of coloured outlines.

The finished monogram may be attached to the cake directly or examples are shown on page 225 of suitable plaques on which to mount them before attaching to the cake.

POSITIONING OF LETTERING

You may occasionally require to arrange lettering other than horizontally or vertically, positioning an inscription on an angle can produce pleasing effects if used correctly. Using lettering at an angle may sometimes be the only way to facilitate an inscription due to the shape, position or size of other decoration being included in the design. The following methods will help you to create attractive curved and angled inscriptions.

Lettering can be placed to appear slanted quite easily on a square or rectangular cake due to the overall shape which determines a level when viewing the cake fig. 174. The slanted lettering effect has still been achieved on a round cake in fig. 175 but because the floral motif fig. 175a has no vertical or horizontal level the cake can be rotated to make the lettering appear horizontal.

FIG. 174

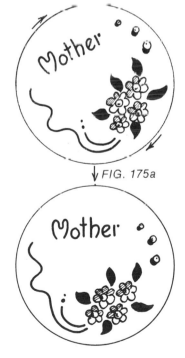

FIG. 175a

FIG. 175

175

Lettering arranged at an angle can be achieved by drawing two lines spaced to the height of the required lettering. These lines may be parallel to each other fig. 176a or graduated as in fig.176b. If lower case lettering is to be included, a third line will be required fig. 176c. Using the base line YZ align a set square and draw in the required vertical lines to form the vertical down strokes of each letter, horizontal strokes and cross-bars are drawn in along the horizontal guidelines.

Note the centre guideline on fig. 176b is gained by using the centre point of the depth or height of each end of the graduation.

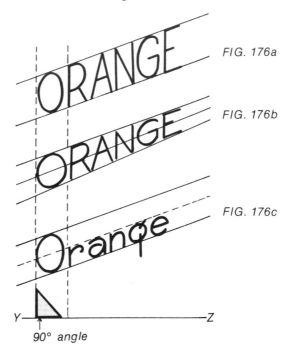

FIG. 176a

FIG. 176b

FIG. 176c

Y   Z

90° angle

Lettering on an irregular curve can be drawn in a similar manner. Draw out the required curve, then make a tracing of the curve and transfer the tracing parallel to the first curve and to the required height of the lettering fig. 177. Proceed as for fig. 176 to draw in the vertical strokes, forming the horizontal strokes along the curves. Fig. 177b shows graduated curved lettering.

Angled lettering on a horizontal plane fig. 178 can be achieved by drawing two horizontally parallel lines (three lines required for lower case). Then using a card template, cut at a right angle (90°) and cut to the required angle of the lettering align the template to the base line and draw in a pencil line along the lettering angle side, move the template along the base line to the width required for the letter and pencil in a second line. Use this 'box' as an outline for the letter, leave the required space and commence with the second letter and so on. Fig. 178f shows some of the more difficult letters to draw at an angle using sub divisions of each 'box' or letter area.

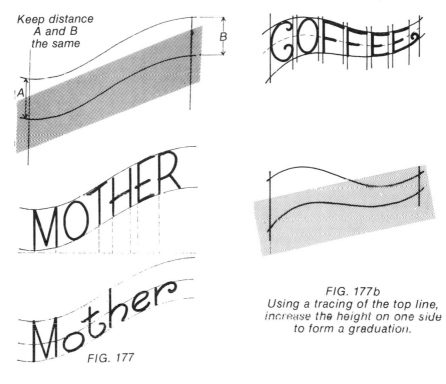

Keep distance A and B the same

FIG. 177

FIG. 177b
Using a tracing of the top line, increase the height on one side to form a graduation.

Card template

a

b

c

d

EASTER

e

ASYRG

f

25abcd

Examples of
lower case
slanted
lettering.

g

FIG. 178

The previous method combined with the method of writing on a curve can be used to produce angled lettering on a curved plane fig 179.

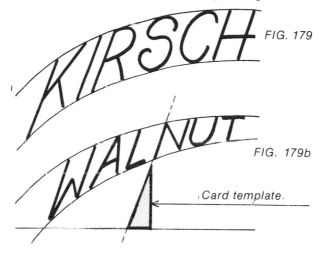

FIG. 179

FIG. 179b

Card template.

Application of lettering inscriptions based on circular or semi-circular arrangements may be required from time to time. Spaced and positioned accurately this type of layout can look particularly attractive around a circular centrepiece feature ornament, painted plaque or a club badge or logo or simply to follow the edge shape of a round cake.

FIG. 180

Fig. 180 shows the plan of a semi-circular arrangement of lettering. Remember when measuring to clear the edge of the cake allowing for piping, run-out linework. Note how all vertical strokes follow the radius of the circle and are radiated from lines meeting at the centrepoint horizontal letter strokes follow the circumference. Use the same method for the top half of a circle.

179

When using a full circle one should decide whether to continue facing the lettering outwards all the way round fig. 181a or split the inscription half way as in fig. 181b. This will depend upon whether the cake will be acceptably pleasing to view from all angles. In my opinion, fig. 181a has an unbalanced effect which is not instantly recognizable.

FIG. 181a   FIG. 181b

To centralize a curved or even a straight word on a cake, do not rely on the often recommended method of dividing the number of letters in the word equally in half, as problems can occur. For instance in the word Birthday which contains eight letters, dividing the word in half would result in the right-hand side being wider than the left. This is due to the fact that the three 'wide' and one thin letter 'I' on the left-hand side do not occupy as much space as the four 'wide' letters on the right-hand side.

FIG. 182

Incorrect.
Centralised by dividing in half
the number of letters within the
word.

Correct.
Centralised by dividing in half
the measured length of the word.

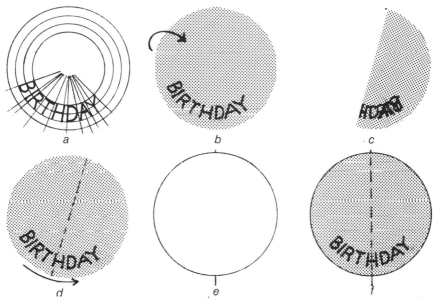

A SIMPLE METHOD TO USE WHEN CENTRALISING WORDS IS SHOWN ABOVE

a. *Draw the required lettering as described in fig. 180 spacing the letters accordingly*

b, *Make a tracing of the inscription and fold in half using the top outward facing*
&   *corners of each end letter as opposites, in this case the top left-hand corner of*
c. *letter 'B' and the top right-hand corner of the letter 'Y'.*

d. *The crease of the greaseproof paper will form the centre line for the inscription.*

e. *Mark a centre (in this case an horizontal line) on the design or cake top.*

f   *Align the crease on the greaseproof paper with the centre line on the design or*
    cake and trace into position.

Examples are illustrated of all types and styles of lettering discussed in this chapter. Please note and remember to keep all vertical strokes accurately vertical and if writing at an angle do not vary the angle throughout the inscription. Letters such as A E R F H B G should have their cross bars in the same position throughout the inscription to give a uniform appearance either near the top, in the centre or near the base of the letter. Also avoid mixing upper and lower case letters in a word, except obviously when using them as capitals. Letters repeated in a word should be kept as the same style - don't have a "y" with a straight tail and one with a curly one in the same word. Finally, a dislike of mine which students new to lettering on cakes will pursue is full stops at the end of a greeting or name, quite unnecessary.

The lettering styles which follow from page 182 to 189 are ideal for compiling your own individual inscriptions and names, all being mainly suited to DIRECT PIPING with the exception of style 2 which could be used for RUN-OUT lettering, or even outlined in chocolate coloured icing or fondant to be filled in with coloured piping jelly or fondant. Lettering style 7 is particularly suited to execution in piping chocolate or fondant, to enable the graduated thick and thin strokes to be piped in a flowing manner.

Birthday *Using style 1*

Birthday *Using style 2*

Birthday *Using style 3*

Birthday *Using style 4*

Birthday ·*Using style 5*

Birthday *Using style 6*

Birthday *Using style 7*

Piped inscriptions.

Style 1

Style 2

Style 3

Style 4

Style 5

Style 6

Style 7

Alphabet for piped inscriptions

Style 1

Style 2

Style 3

Style 4

Style 5

Style 6

Style 7

Alphabet for piped inscriptions

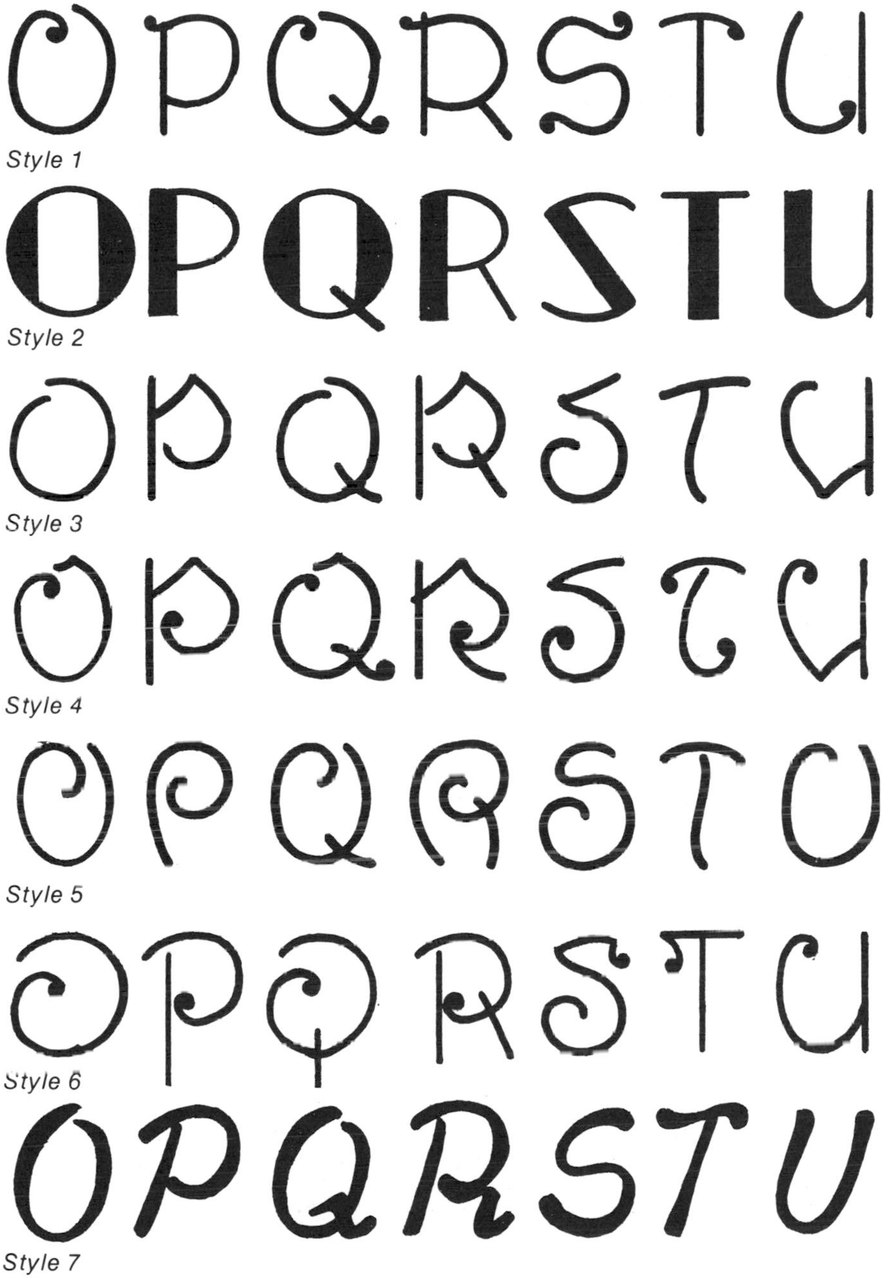

O P Q R S T U

Style 1

O P Q R S T U

Style 2

O P Q R S T U

Style 3

O P Q R S T U

Style 4

O P Q R S T U

Style 5

O P Q R S T U

Style 6

O P Q R S T U

Style 7

Alphabet for piped inscriptions

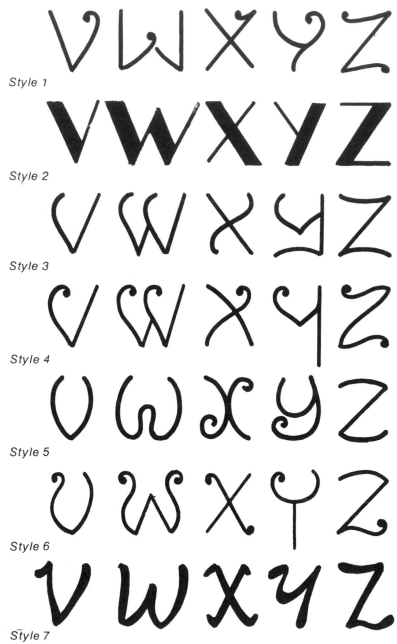

Style 1

Style 2

Style 3

Style 4

Style 5

Style 6

Style 7

Alphabet for piped inscriptions

Style 1

Style 2

Style 3

Style 4

Style 5

Style 6

Style 7

Alphabet for piped inscriptions

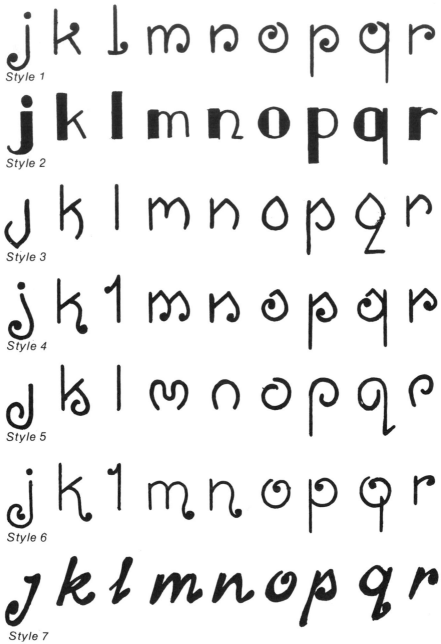

Style 1

Style 2

Style 3

Style 4

Style 5

Style 6

Style 7

Alphabet for piped inscriptions

Style 1

Style 2

Style 3

Style 4

Style 5

Style 6

Style 7

Alphabet for piped inscriptions

To create a more interesting and attractive name or inscription from a basic lettering style, use the last letter such as Y's shown above to add 'curvy' endings and embellishments.

The same extra embellishments can also be used on the first or capital letter of a name or inscription as shown in the selection above.

When drawing your inscription, try linking various letters and words together as shown here.

Lettering suitable for run-out method of application with or without an outline.
Also suitable for stencil type lettering.

191

Script lettering suitable for direct piping.

Lettering suitable for run-out or stencil application.
No real 'ties' have been used to make the style look less like stencil lettering
when applied to the cake surface.

Lower case alphabet for use with previous capital letters.

The following pages provide a most comprehensive range of inscriptions in various styles and sizes which can be adapted to most of the applications described earlier. The range covers celebrations and occasions, names, flavours and seasonal themes. The size of the inscriptions will be exactly right for at least some of your designs and cakes, so trace them directly from the book, other sizes of cakes can be catered for simply by reducing or enlarging the size of a particular inscription accordingly. Enjoy using them!

HAPPY BIRTHDAY

Happy Birthday

Happy Birthday

Happy Birthday

5

Today

A HAPPY BIRTHDAY

HAPPY BIRTHDAY

We wish you ...

Best

Wishes

Happy

Birthday

Happy

Birthday

Have a nice... (0)ELLO

Hello!

Ahoy!

Best Wishes

Get Well With Love

It's your Today Hi there!

MERRY CHRISTMAS

Peace on Earth

Holy Night

Holy Night

Christmas

Christmas Cheer

Christmas

Christmas

198

Rejoice

Christmas

Peace
on
Earth

Christmas

Greetings

Greetings

Christmas

Blessings

Christmas

Greetings

Silent Night

Noel

NOEL

NOEL

EASTER

HAPPY EASTER

HAPPY EASTER

Easter

EASTER

Easter

EASTER

Mother MUM
Mother Mother
Mother Mother
Mum
Mum Father's Day
DAD DADDY
Dad Love Love
Valentine

Congratulations

Congratulations

Congratulations

Congratulations

Congratulations

CONGRATULATIONS

Congratulations

Congratulations

Congratulations

Greetings

GREETINGS

Good Anniversary
Luck Ruby
Silver Silver
Golden Wedding
Engagement Confirmation Retirement
Engagement
Engagement

Christening

It's

NIGELS

Christening

Welcome

WELCOME

Anniversary

Baby

Christening

CHRISTENING

ANDREW
MARTIN
Helen Diana
George Neil
Chris RETA
RODNEY
Alison Sarah
Valerie Ben

JACKIE
DARYL
Russell
Wendy
Geoffrey
Simon
SUSAN
MANDY
TOMMY
Rachel

Orange Lemon Strawberry Cherry Walnut Kirsch RUM HAZELNUT Caramel Choc RUM Pineapple Banana

CHAPTER 11

Prefabricated Decoration

The confectioner will no doubt find the use of prefabricated plaques invaluable, especially during the busy periods when decorative work could eventually result in a lower standard of quality then normal, owing to work pressure and time available at Christmas and Easter time.

The decoration could be prepared by skilled operatives premature to the busy periods, and then easily applied to confectionery by semi-skilled labour, making considerable savings in time and wages.

Prefabricated decoration is by no means new to the confectioner in any way, as it's use as been apparent for many years. The fact is, many bakers tend to neglect this area of finishing and decoration and opt for "bought in" decorations, instead of successfully using it to their advantage. The more common forms used, and still in use are prepared sugarpaste inscription plaques for celebration and fruit gateaux etc. Wedding cake centrepieces even royal icing piped flowers could fall into this category, along with run-outs and several other prepared decorations.

All could easily be hand-made by the confectioner, as well as being purchased via the bakery sundriesman in mass produced form.

Obviously in a commercial situation, any materials which can save time, make profit and still retain the expected standard and quality of the establishment are more than welcome. Prefabricated decoration produced by the confectioner for use on his own products will still reflect the character of the establishment.

Prefabricated decoration "bought in" by the confectioner can in certain instances result in customers loosing faith in the establishment that usually try to give a home-made or even hand-made appearances to their products. In the case of the plant bakers who mass produce confectionery, but rarely spend time with intricate decoration, they have no option but to "buy in" prefabricated decoration such as plastic or paper. The most discerning customer accepts this and would probably purchase her special occasion cakes from the smaller craft bakers.

PREFABRICATED PLAQUES Fig. 184

These can be the same size of the cake top to be decorated or a smaller size fig. 185 to be an integral part of the decoration of a cake base prepared with royal icing, fondant, chocolate, marzipan or buttercream. The edible base would be adorned with any or all of the following, depending on size, lettering and motif (flowers and figures), linework and edging motif.

The plaques would be finished previous to the required date of use and stored carefully. Cakes are then produced up to the decorative stage and the plaques placed on and attached to complete the item as demand requires, therefore eliminating possible wasted time and materials involved in completely finishing the cakes. The plaques not required could then be further stored for a later date, only the base is redundant, and not the time consuming decorative portion, the base would be re-cycled in some way.

FIG. 184
Prefabricated Christmas cake tops - sugarpaste disc with lettering and marzipan motif.

FIG. 184a
Prefabricated christening cake motif sugarpaste oval with piped royal icing stork motif.

FIG. 185
Prefabricated full-relief marzipan animals.

PLAQUE PAINTING

Painting onto cakes is not usually accepted as being a commercially viable method of cake decoration. It is one of the more specialized aspects of cake artistry, creating an extremely high class appearance to the confectionery on which it is applied, providing of course that the application is of a reasonable standard. Depending upon the detail involved, painting on cakes or plaques could be used commercially in the more 'high class' type establishment where the discerning clientel are prepared to pay for quality workmanship and something a little out of the ordinary.

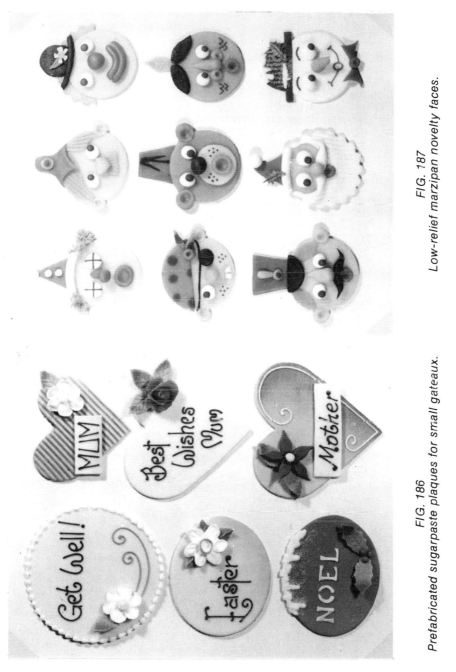

FIG. 187
Low-relief marzipan novelty faces.

FIG. 186
Prefabricated sugarpaste plaques for small gateaux.

Don't be afraid of painting onto royal icing or sugarpaste. The principle is much the same as for painting poster or gouache paint onto paper, with a few exceptions, the main one being paint consistency.

Until one becomes more experienced, there is usually a fear, initially of making a mistake when painting, and as a result the cake being spoilt. Imagine the icing or sugarpaste as art paper and this will help your confidence considerably. A way of avoiding possible mistakes directly onto a royal iced surface, is to paint your chosen design onto a prepared plaque of sugarpaste or preferably run-out royal icing, which is then positioned and attached to the cake and can be finished by a simple dot design surrounding the edge or a build-up of linework, even a run-out frame sprayed gold or silver if the occasion allows.

Several examples of shapes for such plaques are illustrated on page 227, choose one or two suitably shaped to compliment the composition of your proposed painting, always prepare at least one extra plaque as a spare on which to practice first. The reason I stated a preference for a run-out as opposed to a sugarpaste plaque, is simply the far superior surface obtained by the former type, on which to paint.

Painted plaques for various occasions and themes.
To add more relief on painted plaques, certain parts in the foreground could be run-out and attached separately. For instance on the plaques shown, the arms of the sportsmen, the wing of the stork and the holly leaves near the robin could all be executed in this manner.

As you will appreciate, the surface of correctly dried run-outs has a smooth semi-glossy surface, ideal for the smooth application of paint, whereas a conventional royal iced cake surface or indeed the surface of sugarpaste, even when polished have a more open, slightly coarse, more porous surface, sufficient to allow a certain amount of 'drag' when using a paint brush and a potential risk of paint absorption. Bearing in mind these points it would therefore be advisable if, what is termed a 'directly painted' cake surface is to be produced to pay particular attention to the final coatings of icing, using a soft, rested icing to attain a fine surface on which to paint.

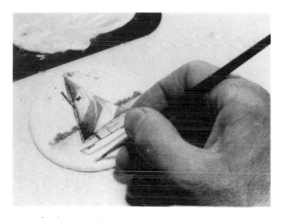

An interesting sea or water effect can
be achieved by using a paintbrush
to apply softened royal icing in white
and various shades of blue.

Depending obviously on the nature of the composition and detail, one has to first determine where to commence application of the paint. It can simply be a matter of painting in the palest tones, building up to shadows and detail, with or without an outline. In the case of some figures or scenes where a background shading is required, a stencil or template image of the unshaded area needs to be cut and positioned on the cake surface or plaque. The background or shaded area can then be applied by means of an aerograph spray gun (pen) with the colour or colours to achieve the required effect. The template is then removed to reveal the area to be painted i.e. church or figure.

Note:
Masking of cake tops and sides will be required to avoid unwanted settlement of sprayed colour.

Outlines around paintings are a personal choice, I prefer any natural scene or figure with little or no outline, however, on cartoon type figures and animals or where outlines are essential such as on 'Club Badges' or Coat of Arms a dark chocolate colour or black outline makes the image more eyecatching.

To prepare paint for application, always start with a base of white compound, edible white compound is available to the confectioner. If it is anticipated that the plaque or cake surface will not be eaten, poster or gouache can be used, the small amount of usually non-toxic paint should be quite safe. If necessary, explain to the customer or attach a label to the cake box warning that the plaque is not edible.

Mix the white compound with a little water until a working consistency is attained, because of the easily dissolvable, porous nature of the surfaces to be painted avoid using too much water when diluting the compound, also take into account the addition of more liquid in the form of edible food colourings. The food colourings are added to the white mixture in the same way that colour pigments of poster and gouache are added to white paint for painting on paper. If however, a deep colour is required for instance Christmas red or dark chocolate then use a paste or compound type edible colour, otherwise the amount of liquid colour required to achieve a deep colour could probably dilute the paint too much.

Apply the paint carefully, remembering not to apply too much at once, this would result in the sugar dissolving and forming hollows in the surface, sugarpaste however will tolerate slightly more dilute paint before dissolving.

Build-up the areas gradually rather than flooding the surface with moisture, keeping the paint brush relatively dry. Far better results will be obtained by applying the paint fairly slow with a dryish brush as opposed to trying to cover an area quickly with a wet brush. Under normal room temperatures the painted surface will dry quite quickly, enabling further detail, shading and outlining to be carried out.

Outlining can be executed by means of a fine line painted using a number 0, 00, or 000 brush in a darker colour than that of the base colour, or as a general application in a chocolate colour (using compound or paste type colours) or with edible black coloured compound carefully diluted with a little water. Also available for outlining or indeed for any colour application are edible food colour fine felt tip pens.

a

b

c

d

e

*PAINTED TEDDY BEAR PLAQUE
SUITABLE FOR A
CHRISTENING CAKE.*

a. *Design outline.*

b. *Base colour applied.*

c. *Applying shading, an imaginary
arrow will help you to remember
direction of light.*

d. *Detail and features painted on to
complete the plaque.*

e. *Optional, a fine outline around
the figure.*

217

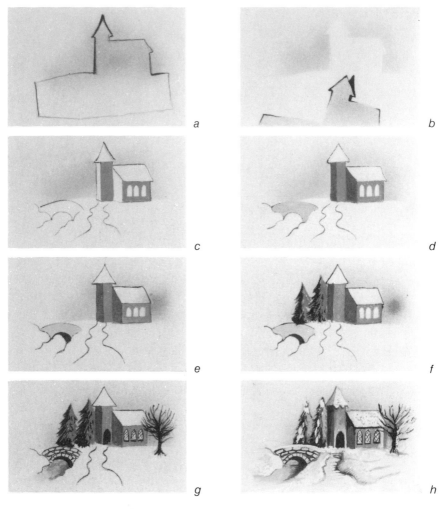

a.

b.

c.

d.

e.

f.

g.

h.

CHRISTMAS CHURCH SCENE DIRECTLY PAINTED

a. Prepared paper outline template to mask off picture area.
b. Removal of mask to reveal prepared painting area.
c. Outline of picture applied and some colour painted in.
d. Bridge and darker or shaded part of church painted in.
e. Further sprayed colour to act as a "filler" and background to trees.
f. Trees painted in.
g. Church windows, stonework on bridge and water painted in, note the use of two shades for water.
   Softened royal icing brushed on church roof and foreground to depict snow, sprinkle the icing with caster sugar to create a frosty effect.

PREFABRICATED MODELS

Prepared off pieces for the sugarpaste church.

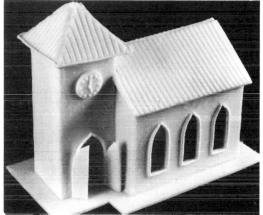

The assembled sugarpaste church.

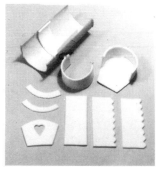

Prepared off pieces for the sugarpaste cradle

The assembled sugarpaste cradle.

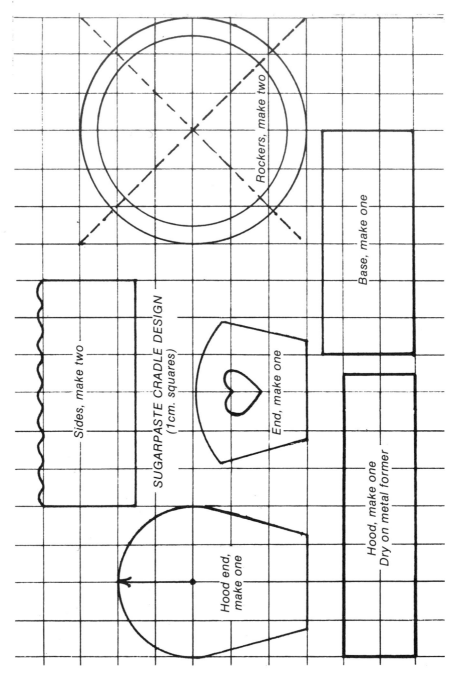

Rockers, make two

Base, make one

Sides, make two

SUGARPASTE CRADLE DESIGN
(1cm. squares)

End, make one

Hood, make one
Dry on metal former

Hood end, make one

Tower roof, make 4

Tower, make 4
(3 plain, 1 with door)

SUGARPASTE CHURCH DESIGN
Enlarge or reduce using methods on page 65.

Ends, make 1 with window
and 1 without.

Roof, make two
(leave plain or rib roll, stipple texture etc.)

Sides, make two

PREFABRICATED BADGES

Using the principles of run-out work, badges and logos for presentation cakes can be produced.

By kind permission of The Boots Company PLC, Nottingham.

By kind permission of C. & A.

Prepare the design from an original drawing, reducing or enlarging using the technique described on page 65.

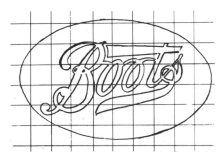

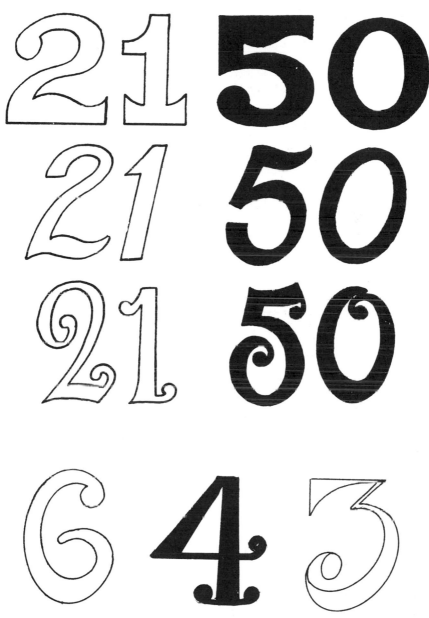

*Suitable for tracing - Numerical outlines for birthday/anniversary cake ornaments.
Note: The style of 2 and 5 on each line are matched to produce a 25.*

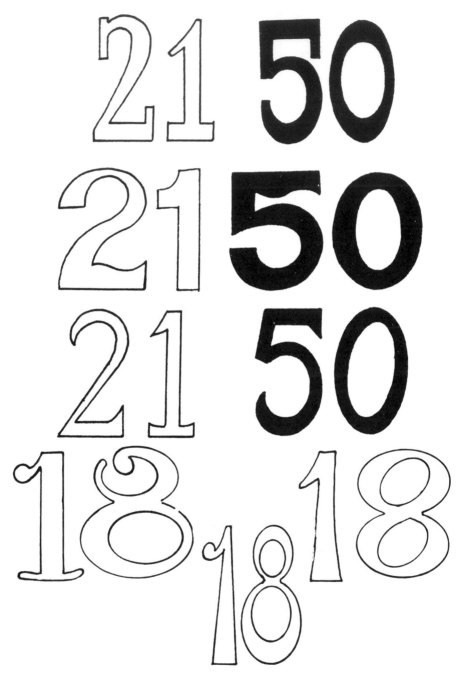

224

More outlines for ornament or painted plaques.

Assembled run-out 21's and plaques. Note the use of coloured outlines and gold/silver spray.

225

CHOCOLATE DECORATIONS

Cut chocolate pieces

CHOCOLATE DECORATIONS

a. Plain chocolate disc spun with milk chocolate.

b. Criss cross spun chocolate.

c. Circular spun chocolate.

d. Plain chocolate allowed to set, cover with milk chocolate - comb scrape - cut out into shapes when set.

e. Chocolate sprinkled with nibbed almonds or green decor.

f. Chocolate disc gently pressed onto piped buttercream rosette and then reversed and positioned onto rosette.

| a | b | c | d |

PIPED CHOCOLATE PIECES FOR GATEAUX AND TORTE SEGMENT DECORATION

a. Plain chocolate base, milk chocolate drop on top.

b. Chocolate drop with 3 hazelnuts.

c. Milk chocolate base, plain chocolate top.

d. Chocolate drop with walnut half.

Milk chocolate

Plain chocolate

Designs for piped chocolate pieces.

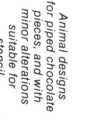

Animal designs
for piped chocolate
pieces, and with
minor alterations
suitable for
stencil
application.

Designs for piped chocolate pieces.

228

CHAPTER 12

Stencilling

Stencilling can be defined as applying paint or other coloured substances through a design of cut-outs in a sheet of paper, card, parchment or metal to leave an impression on the surface below. The technique of stencilling can be applied to a wide range of surfaces such as fabric and textiles, plaster and ceramic tiles, furniture to name but a few. Not used nowadays by the confectionery as much as it could be, although one good example of stencilling used by the baker is the paper doyley dusted with cocoa or icing sugar to leave the doyley pattern on the cake surface. There is however a great potential for decorative work in the form of motifs, cake tops and side designs, lettering and inscriptions in several mediums used by the cake decorator which can be stencilled as opposed to the use of piped or cut-out decorations. As with all other techniques there are advantages and disadvantages, the main benefits being time and labour savings once the stencil has been produced, along with the fact that semi-skilled operatives can carry out the techniques with success, opposed to the degree of skill required to handle a piping bag.

A stencil of lettering for example could be a little more elaborately designed than the lettering a baker would normally pipe, conventional lettering can easily be piped onto a cake surface and as there is little extra time involved desiging and cutting, more elaborate motifs and letters could be used for stencil work. Sometimes a bold abstract type of design can be produced and after application onto the cake top additional decoration can be used to increase the detail once a basic stencil shape has been applied to the product.

This form of cake art could then cover a wide spectrum of requirements from a basic commercial type design to the more intricate detailed work used by the exhibition cake decorator. The simpler designs would obviously appeal more to the master baker in terms of costs, and could be of great commercial value as once the stencil has been designed and cut, provided a suitable material is used it can be used over and over again.

Some of the larger bakery ingredient manufacturers have supplied bakers with plastic stencils bearing attractive seasonal designs which are easy to use and maintain, however the baker round the corner may be using these same stencils, so individual creativity will be required to offer your customers something different.

STENCIL DESIGNING

In designing stencils we usually have to include what are known as 'ties', these are the sections joining or keeping the stencil together. Without ties portions of the stencil when cut, would fall out, this in turn would result in the definition of the design being affected. Ties should be used as cleverly as possible so that they seem to be part of the design, when in actual fact they will be holding the finished unit together.

The initial design should consist only of a silhouette type drawing of the original. This can then be broken down into sections, the sections being made at some point where they can be used as ties. Using the leaf in fig. 188a as an example we start off with an outline of the leaf (this could be used as a simple stencil) next we can add a little detail in the form of a centre vein fig. 188b, and finally adding even more interest to the stencil the side veins are included.

FIG. 188

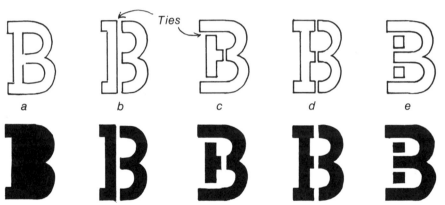

Example showing design of stencil type lettering using 'TIES'

a. No. 'TIES' have been used here, therefore when the letter is cut-out the inner portions cannot be held in, resulting in a bold block letter. The lack of detail would make this style of lettering ideal for a childs cake.

b, c, d, and e all have 'TIES' incorporated within the design, thus when cut-out retain a more detailed letter.

Even so the same letter could be designed for stencil work without using such intricate 'TIES'. This in my opinion produces letters which don't immediately strike you as being stencilled. All letters of the alphabet can be treated in this way see pages 191, 193, 194 for full alphabet.

CONSTRUCTING A STENCIL Fig. 189

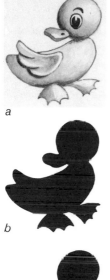

a

a. Prepare the picture to be produced as a stencil by drawing to the correct size required. (Reduction and enlargement page 65). The picture should be as simple as possible, preferably a line drawing with not too much detail. The image should first be outlined around the most important or relevant features, ignoring shading and unnecessary detail.

b

b. If we were to cut out each individual section previously outlined in fig. 189a the stencil would be disintegrated into small sectional pieces unsuitable as a stencil, in effect producing a "jigsaw". The simplest stencil therefore would obviously be a strict outline of the image (opposite). Using this method all detail is lost as the result is a silhouette type stencil. The example of the duck fortunately works quite well as a silhouette and is relatively easily recognised, other figures however, may not be reproduced quite so easily without significant alterations to the outline.

c

c. During the construction of the stencil we can include 'TIES' as described earlier to create more detail. The stencil shown has become more interesting and meaningful by the inclusion of ties. Ties in this example are used around the beak, feet, and wing of the duck. The wing however, could prove to be flimsy and prone to damage quite easily, this would depend on the material being used to produce the stencil, card would tear or break at the join of the wing after only a few uses, whereas a metal or plastic stencil would be stronger and more durable.

d

d. The wing in this example has been cut differently to make a stronger stencil, this has inevitably resulted in the stencil taking on a more solid appearance. This can be useful to indicate the difference of what should be solid and what should be more open or lighter in order to convey the correct image of the surface or material being depicted within the stencil.

An attempt has been made to indicate the ducks eye, as an example how not to use ties (unless it is a last resort to be able to include a particular detail). The line (tie) detracts from the image and professionalism of the design.

e. This final example has been constructed with a more delicate and detailed approach. Construction is based on the outlines of the body and head being incorporated in the design as the actual stencil. The use of such outlines has enabled us to include the eye without a tie, note also the extra detail in the wing and the bottom of the beak. Tufts of grass have also been included to complete the picture.

e

Once the stencil is designed a tracing should be made of it onto the chosen stencil material.

STENCIL MATERIALS

Normally one would want to use a stencil several times, it is not such a viable proposition to spend time designing and cutting a stencil to use for one operation only. So we select a material which can be used repeatedly without easily becoming damaged:

Thin card or even "cakebox"	Suitable only for a short run of stencilling, is not water resistant therefore unable to be washed.
Parchment-oil impregnated paper	Easy to cut using a blade or craft knife. Being water resistant can be washed successfully and re-used.
Celluloid and acetate	Can be more difficult to cut, but is easy to maintain. Can also be used to stencil onto for shiny flower petals etc.
Plastic, wood and metal	Long lasting and easily maintainable but would probably have to be professionally cut to be successful.

Washing of stencils, especially parchment should be carried out very carefully so as not to damage the sometimes extremely thin cut sections.

It is best to let water flow over the stencil until all the icing or colour is removed, then should be dried and stored flat ready for the next use.

To obtain a really neat design cut-out the stencil (parchment or acetate) using a sharp craft knife or blade rather than scissors, use a flat piece of wood under the stencil whilst cutting.

USING THE STENCIL

Having designed and cut the stencil we can now place it on the surface to be decorated this could be fondant, chocolate, or royal icing coated cake. Keeping the stencil still we would then apply a suitable medium that would compliment the rest of the cake in terms of flavour, texture, and also using a suitable colour. This could be in the form of sprayed colour or a medium spread over the stencil, after which we remove the stencil to leave the impression on the surface below.

Using a stencil with royal icing.

Some mediums: Royal icing.
Colour sprayed using an aerograph.
Edible colour spray.

Royal icing Various colours - create a raised effect.

Sprayed colour Quicker method, using an aerograph spray gun or a modern edible colour aerosol spray.

Buttercreams Various colours - again creating a raised effect.

Dusting Using cocoa powder on a light surface and icing sugar on darker surfaces.

Butterfly

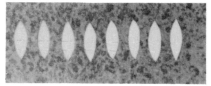

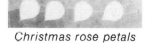

Christmas rose petals

Lilly type petal for royal icing centrepiece.

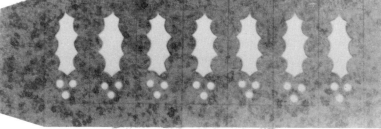

Full stencil for layer cake top.

EXAMPLES OF PARCHMENT STENCILS

Stencil designs

Stencil designs

Stencil designs.
The Christmas stencil (top right) is ideal to use stencilled onto a sugarpaste disc to make an effective prefabricated decoration.

Snowman (bottom right). Snow could be white icing bulbs piped directly onto the cake surface after the stencil had been applied, instead of being an integral part of the stencil design.

EASTER

EASTER

Happy

Birthday

Hazelnut

Hazelnut

Daniel Daniel

Stencil designs

Stencil designs

Stencil designs

Stencil designs - floral themes

Outlines for stencilled Butterflies

Birthday cake stencil design for full cake top.

The stencil - cut and prepared from parchment paper ready for use.

The finished cake. Chocolate fondant covering with coffee coloured rib-rolled marzipan semi-circles.

Stencil design: Pale blue space ship, white 'space age' lettering, yellow star and red-orange and yellow flame effect. All in royal icing. The 'Have a . . .' and 'Birthday' lettering are directly piped onto the cake using orange coloured royal icing, this gives a more personalised hand finished appearance as opposed to only the stencil being used.

CHAPTER 13

Flowers and Leaves

USING FLOWERS

Flowers have always been used extensively by the confectioner, they can be incorporated into cake designs in numerous ways. Flowers for confectionery use can be silk, wafer paper, plastic or may be produced by the confectioner in the form of cut and moulded marzipan, sugarpaste or royal icing. Royal iced flowers can be made by various methods including stencilling, run-out, or piping. Chocolate outlines filled in with coloured piping jellies also make attractive floral decorations usually to be piped onto plaques or directly onto cake tops. Flower colours range from the palest tint through to very strong colours, flower colours are natural colours and therefore the confectionery designer needn't worry too much about possible discordant effects when using these vivid colours, except in extreme instances of combination, and can easily be incorporated into a design without appearing discordant, the reason being that we accept these natural colours belong to the flowers themselves and not to the cake itself.

Leaves should be studied carefully before attempting to use floral decoration. There are long narrow leaves these belong to the daffodil, iris, and tulip type flowers, then we have the oval type leaf which belongs to the rose, fuchsia etc. The former leaves being without veins and the latter having veins. Study also leaf edges which vary tremendously, some plain, some with a serrated edge, not to mention all the various outline shapes. Leaf joints to main stems should also be noted, along with the natural straight or curved form of the stem which should be carried through onto the design. So often one sees on cakes, flowers with the wrong leaves or stem shape through not copying natures growth pattern of the flower. The exception to the rule of copying nature would obviously be if the confectioner wishes to produce his own imaginary flower and leaf designs.

a   b   c   d   e

a. *Cut chocolate pieces with piping jelly centre.*
b. *Split almonds, partly dipped in chocolate, cut glace cherry centre.*
c. *Green jelly or angelica, cut glace cherry centre.*
d. *Piped and filled chocolate.*
e. *Piped chocolate outline filled-in with piping jelly.*

Piped royal icing pansies, leaves outlined in chocolate and filled in with green piping jelly.

Arrangement of piped royal icing daisies.

When using piped or moulded forms of natures flowers, pipe the stems to resemble their natural growth habit, i.e. curved or straight. With imaginary type flowers such as cut chocolate or split almond formations any shape or form of stem could be used providing it compliments the arrangement. The form and arrangement of stems will sometimes be limited by the shape of the cake top and the space available. A round cake for instance will lend itself particularly well to curvy type groupings, whereas layer or bar type cakes can carry straight stems easier, square cakes will take both curved and straight, this is not a strict rule to adhere to but a guideline until experience is gained as any shape of stem can be used on any shape of cake and still produce excellently balanced designs.

After arranging the stems, take care to position the flowers so as to appear natural, and not all on the same plane, this applies to both natural and imaginary type flowers. To explain this, below we see two flower arrangements, one with all the flowers on the same horizontal plane, and the other more acceptable naturally arranged type of grouping using varying levels or heights for each flower.

All flowers arranged on same level or plane.

Using similar stem curves a more natural and informal appearance is achieved by arranging the flowers on varying levels.

243

The number of flowers used will be governed by the area of available space in proportion with the size of the cake, the size of each individual flower and whether any other decoration is to be incorporated within the design, such as an inscription plaque. Whatever the eventual total number of flowers is, a more natural appearance will be achieved using the nearest odd number, exceptions to this occur for instance on equally numbered segmented torte or layer cakes, the same plane may have to be used also for each fower on segmented designs and circular arrangements.

An equal number of flowers used in the arrangement.

A more natural grouping is achieved by using an uneven number of flowers

Using the same plane or level for each flower is sometimes inevitable on most segmented type cakes, such as torten and layer cakes. Another method of arrangement would be to vary the flower levels on alternate segments.

Two design layout techniques widely used by the confectioner can be seen here being used to display flowers as a decorative theme.

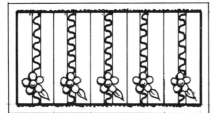

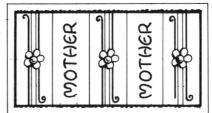

Design repetition.
Segmented layer or bar cake with the same design in each section.

Design alternation.
Segmented layer or bar cake with two alternating sectional designs.

244.

To obtain a more consistent shape within the design of a flower we can combine geometric principles and the techniques of tracing. Most open flowers can be based on a circle, if we then divide the circle each segment can be used to contain a drawing or outline of a single petal, repeated in each of the other segments by tracing to form an accurate flower drawing.

All the flowers shown may be reproduced in most edible materials associated with this type of small decoration. Methods could include run-sugar stencilling, piped royal icing and piped or cut chocolate, even piped outlines filled in with coloured piping jellies.

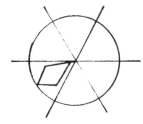  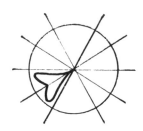

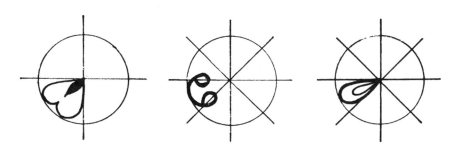

Floral motif and leaf designs suitable for side panels or royal iced cakes and inclusion in cut-outs or on surface of run-out collars.

247

A selection of leaf and stem designs are shown here and on the following page.
Adapt these basic shapes to suit your requirements, tracing direct from the book.
Most are suited to various methods of application i.e. run-out directly piped, piped
outline filled in with piping jelly, moulded and cut-out etc.

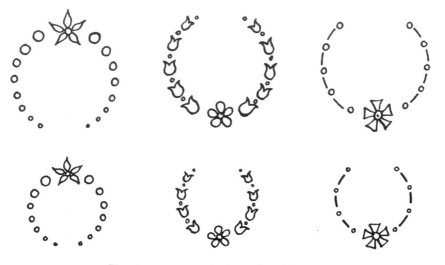

Floral arrangements for cake side panel.

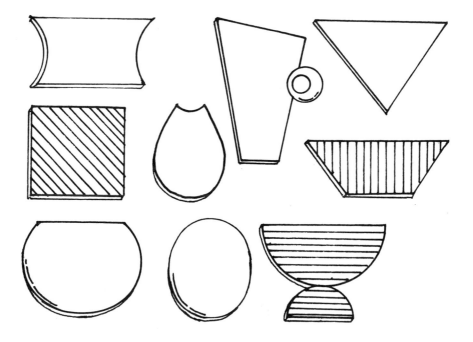

A selection of vase shapes suitable for cut-out sugarpaste and marzipan to be used when arranging edible flowers for cake to designs.

Selection of wavy filler lines and foliage type designs.

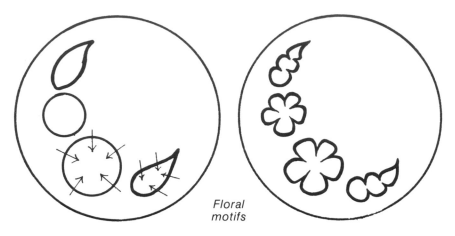

Floral motifs

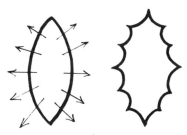

Holly leaf

Designs using marble icing technique.

Thick lines indicate coloured icing piped directly onto still soft water icing or fondant - arrows indicate direction of pull with knife point or skewer.

Christmas layer cake.

Gateaux with space for greeting.

Fuchsia

Christmas Rose and Holly

Christmas Rose, Fir Cone and Holly

Daisy and Violet

Daffodil and Violet

Bunch of Violets

Daffodil, Catkins, Pussy Willow and Violet

Pansies

Sweet Pea

Roses

CHAPTER 14

The Aerograph

The aerograph is a piece of apparatus mainly used by the poster writer and graphic designer, however, it has become accepted as an important part of the designer/confectioners range of equipment and utensils.

It provides a means of applying delicate or strong tints and shades of colour in reasonably large areas but more usefully for small intricate parts of edible decoration and on a wide range of surfaces.

The uses for the imaginative confectioner are wide and varied, among the more common applications are attractively shaded backgrounds for plaque or cake top paintings to represent sky, grass or simply a suitable colour to give a sense of distance to the painting. For smaller areas it lends itself to the colouring of cheeks, blushes and complexions on figures and animals, cartoons etc.

Many people consider the use of the aerograph to be one of the more difficult techniques to be mastered by the confectioner. It is a specialist piece of equipment and requires understanding and a thorough knowledge of the correct use, and equally important the correct cleaning and regular maintenance.

As with most techniques, experience will be the governing influence on the efficient use and ability to control the flow and direct the fine, small amount of colour simultaneously in what are usually relatively confined spaces. In the early stages of use a practice is always beneficial before spraying on the cake, which most probably has taken several hours to prepare, and could be spoiled within seconds. Practice on paper or better still a spare piece of the same material to be sprayed, essentially the same colour, on which to view the finished application, to avoid any deception of the resulting dried colour. Obviously some background colours will not accept and reproduce colours exactly.

The aerograph spray gun (sometimes referred to as a pen or brush) can be of the static type, which uses a large electrically operated air compressor usually housed beneath a spray booth or cubicle to prevent coloured mist settling in unwanted places. Then there are small portable electric compressors which are considerably less expensive and have the advantage of being able to use the unit in different areas. The simplest and cheapest of all systems is the use of an aerosol canister containing the compressed air, which last long enough for most types of work, and does not require electricity. The main advantage I have found where facilities are limited, using this system is convenient for demonstrations in halls etc. When using the canister system beware of the supply finishing unexpectedly which could spoil a cake top when the colour spatters.

Applying colour for stencil work.

Using a masking shape to spray a coloured background previous to painting a scene or figure.

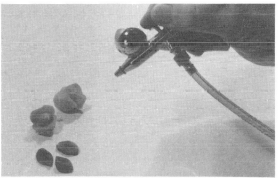

Tinting petal and leaf edges on marzipan roses.

Tinting marzipan fruits.

SOME USES FOR THE AEROGRAPH SPRAY.

257

Designs and Motifs

Layer cake tops.

259

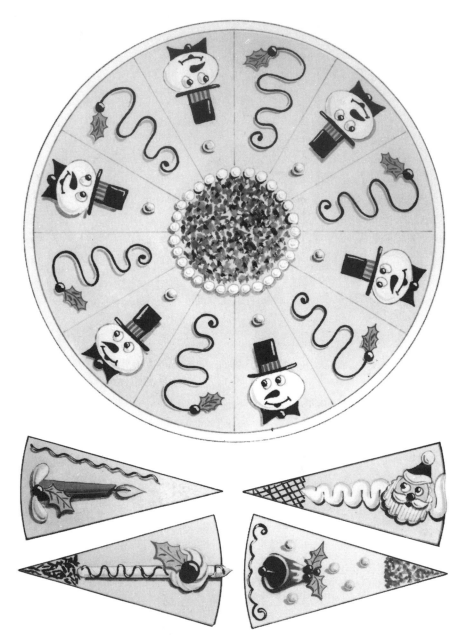

Christmas torten.

Heart designs (see page 36 Symmetrical Motifs).

Valentine and Easter Cake Designs

Mothers Day designs.

Fathers Day designs.

Christening motifs.

Easter torte segments.

Easter motifs.

a   b   c   d

e   f   g   h

i   j   k   l

TORTEN CENTRE DECORATION

a. Centre masking of roasted nibbed (or flaked) almonds.

b. Spun chocolate - one direction, green decor.

c. Spun chocolate - criss cross fashion.

d. Spun chocolate - circular motion.

e. Dredge of sieved jap crumbs.

f. Rib rolled fluted marzipan disc.

g. Sugarpaste disc with inscription.

h. Plain chocolate (set) spread with milk chocolate and comb scraped, cut-out disc as shown. Plain and milk colours may be reversed.

i. Piped chocolate piece or piped and baked choux paste decoration.

j. Dredge of icing sugar or cocoa powder (depending on base colour used).

k. Spiral of buttercream or dairy cream, frozen, peeled off waxed paper and placed onto cake top.

l. Centre masking of chocolate shavings or vermicelli.

268

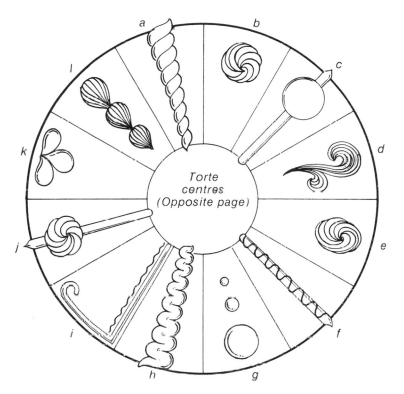

BASIC PIPING LAYOUTS FOR TORTEN DESIGN

a. *Tapered rope of cream.*

b. *Rosette of cream (star tube).*

c. *Line of cream (¼″) and plain bulb.*

d. *S scroll type design.*

e. *Oval shaped rosette.*

f. *Line of cream with chocolate wavy line.*

g. *Graduated plain bulbs.*

h. *Tapered zig-zag design, using plain tube.*

i. *Piped line and wavy line.*

j. *Plain line and rosette.*

k. *Three plain bulbs or shell shapes.*

l. *Graduated shells.*

Use these basic layouts in conjunction with motifs, fruits, nuts and piped or cut pieces etc.

Halloween motifs and stencilled Halloween designs with directly piped lettering.

Bonfire/November 5th motifs and designs.

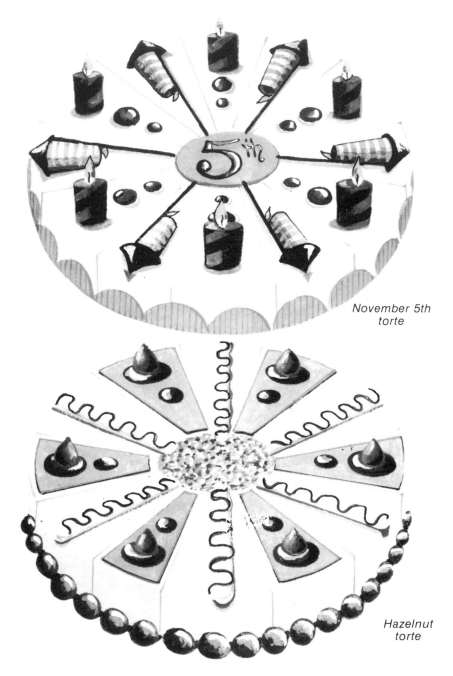

*November 5th
torte*

*Hazelnut
torte*

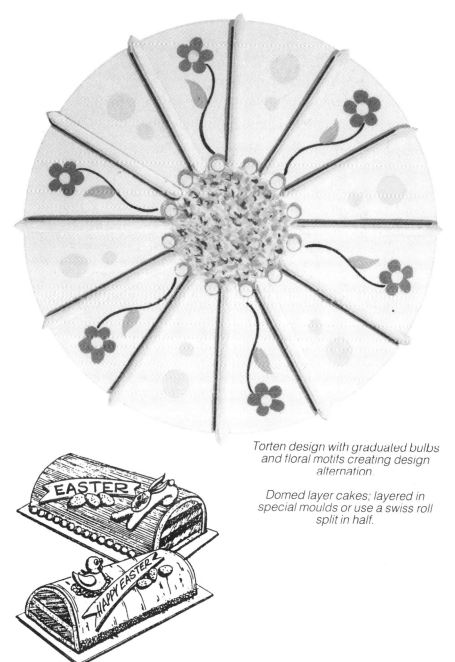

Torten design with graduated bulbs
and floral motifs creating design
alternation.

Domed layer cakes; layered in
special moulds or use a swiss roll
split in half.

273

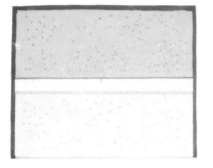
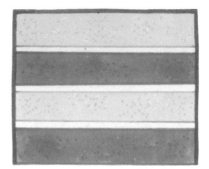

End elevations for layer and bar cakes, showing the creative layering of genoese and cream to produce interesting interiors.

274

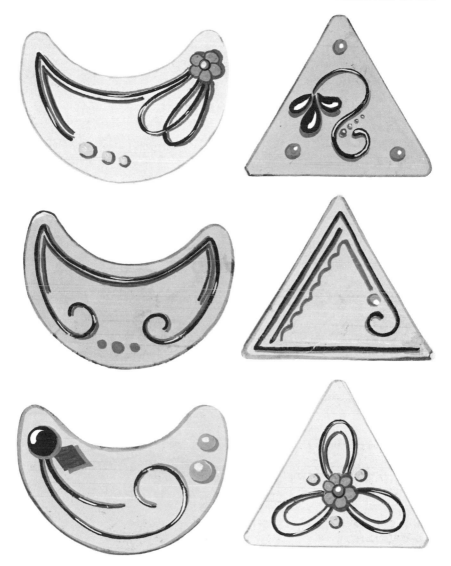

Fondant fancy designs. Illustrating the use of piped linework. See page 91.

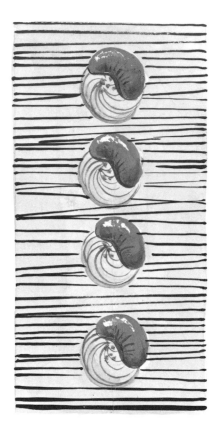

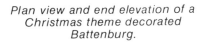

Plan view and end elevation of a Christmas theme decorated Battenburg.

Plan view and end elevation of a swiss roll, decorated with mandarin oranges and spun chocolate lines. Filling; Cream and chopped fruit.

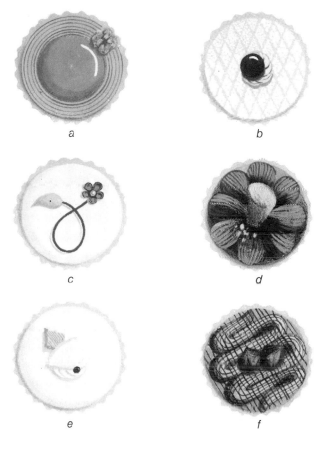

FRANGIPAN FANCY DESIGNS

a. Ring of coffee buttercream piped with a star tube centre filled with coffee fondant, broken walnut.

b. Mask top with Kirsch flavoured cream, dredge with icing sugar and mark into a diamond pattern using the back of a knife. Cream rosette and half glace cherry.

c. Flood top with pale green fondant, pipe curved stem design with fine choc fondant line. Sugar violet and leaf to complete. Leaf could be piping jelly.

d. Chocolate cream shells piped into centre, white marzipan stem and a touch of green nib. Produces a 'mushroom' effect.

e. Flood top with pale lemon fondant, rosette of lemon cream, quarter segment of jelly lemon slice and an angelica diamond.

f. Zig-zag pattern of praline flavoured cream piped with a star tube, spin top with fine lines of chocolate and finish with two roasted whole hazelnuts.

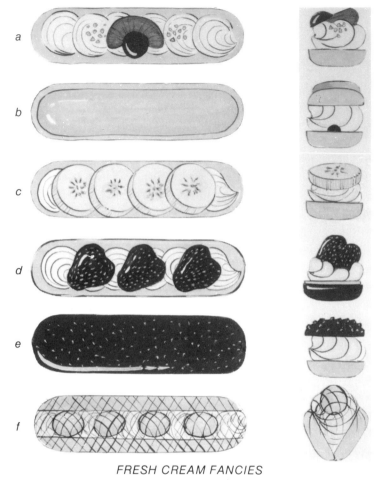

FRESH CREAM FANCIES

All using sponge finger bases

a.   Piped rope of dairy cream, mandarin orange segments, half glace cherry and green decor.

b.   Top sponge finger iced with pink fondant, filling; raspberry jam and piped rope of dairy cream.

c.   Piped rope of dairy cream, glazed banana slices.

d.   Half choux paste eclair shell dipped in melted chocolate, fresh strawberry halves arranged on a piped rope of dairy cream.

e.   Top sponge finger apricot glazed, sprinkle with crushed croquant or roasted nibbed hazelnuts or almonds - enrobe in chocolate.

f.   Sandwich two sponge fingers with dairy cream and decorate with green grape halves and spun chocolate.

Clown motif suitable for
cut marzipan.

Party cakes

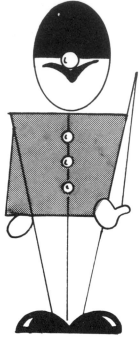

Cut sugarpaste low relief
soldier motif.

"Happy Retirement"
gardening motif.

"Your Engaged"

"Exam Success" Owl motif,
note the use of heart shape
for face.

"Good Luck" motif.

Eye positions and mouths

Noses

Moustache and beard

Cut marzipan   Cut marzipan   Piped   Cut marzipan

Hairstyles

LOW RELIEF MARZIPAN FACES
Various facial expressions, and features to experiment with, when designing faces for motifs.

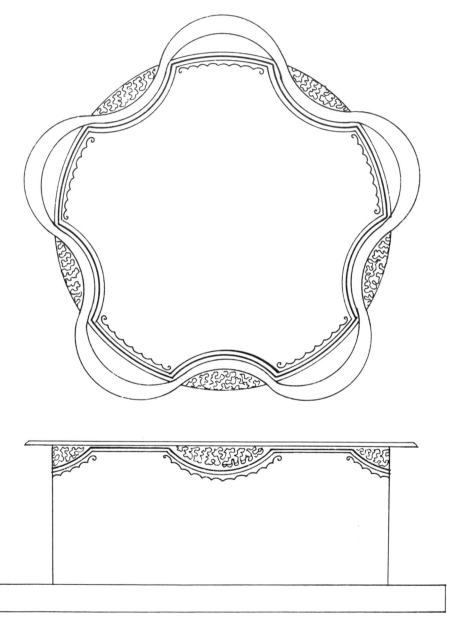

A delicate 'open' run-out collar design. Created to emphasize the top edge of the cake, featuring fine piped filigree work carried from the top surface down onto the side.

NOTES

Index